Modifying Schoolwork

Teachers' Guides to Inclusive Practices

Modifying Schoolwork

Second Edition

by

Rachel Janney, Ph.D.
Radford University
Radford, Virginia

and

Martha E. Snell, Ph.D.
University of Virginia
Charlottesville

·PAUL·H·
BROOKES
PUBLISHING Co.®

Baltimore • London • Sydney

Paul H. Brookes Publishing Co.
Post Office Box 10624
Baltimore, Maryland 21285-0624

www.brookespublishing.com

Typeset by Barton Matheson Willse & Worthington, Baltimore, Maryland.
Manufactured in the United States of America by
Versa Press, East Peoria, Illinois.

Second printing, June 2006.

All of the vignettes in this book are composites of the authors' actual
experiences. In all instances, names have been changed; in some instances,
identifying details have been altered to protect confidentiality.

Library of Congress Cataloging-in-Publication Data

Janney, Rachel.
   Modifying schoolwork / by Rachel Janney and Martha E. Snell.—2nd ed.
     p.   cm.—(Teachers' guides to inclusive practices)
   Includes bibliographical references and index.
   ISBN-13: 978-1-55766-706-9 (papercover/layflat)
   ISBN-10: 1-55766-706-3 (papercover/layflat)
   1. Inclusive education—United States—Planning. 2. Children with
disabilities—Education—United States—Planning. 3. Classroom
management—United States. I. Snell, Martha E. II. Title. III. Series.
LC1201.J26   2004
371.9'046—dc21   2004014900

British Library Cataloguing in Publication data are available from the British Library.

Contents

About the Authors

Rachel Janney, Ph.D., is Professor in the Special Education Department at Radford University in Virginia. She has worked with, and on behalf of, children and adults with disabilities in a number of roles, including special education teacher, educational consultant, researcher, and teacher educator. She received her master's degree from Syracuse University and her doctorate from the University of Nebraska–Lincoln. Dr. Janney now teaches coursework in the special education teacher preparation program at Radford University, specializing in the area of cognitive disabilities. She also supervises student interns and student teachers in a number of schools that have a firm commitment to the full inclusion of all students. Dr. Janney serves as Co-Director of Radford University's Training and Technical Assistance Center, which provides a variety of services and resources to special education teams in school divisions throughout southwest Virginia.

Martha E. Snell, Ph.D., is Professor in the Curry School of Education at the University of Virginia where she has taught since 1973. Her focus is special education and, specifically, the preparation of teachers of students with mental retardation and severe disabilities and young children with disabilities. Prior to completing her doctoral degree in special education at Michigan State University, she worked with children and adults with disabilities as a residential child care worker, a teacher, and a provider of technical assistance to school and residential programs. In addition to teaching courses at the undergraduate and graduate levels, she currently directs the graduate program in severe disabilities and coordinates the special education program, serves on the boards of several community agencies serving people with disabilities, and is an active member of the American Association on Mental Retardation and TASH.

Dr. Janney and coauthor Dr. Snell have conducted several research projects in inclusive schools and classrooms. These projects have studied the ways that special and general educators work together to design and implement modifications and accommodations for students with disabilities in inclusive settings. Both authors are frequent presenters of workshops on topics related to successful inclusive education.

Acknowledgments

This book adapts and builds on the work of many other educators, administrators, and parents who have found effective ways to design schoolwork for students who have an array of abilities and needs. We are particularly grateful for the ideas provided by the work of Alison Ford, Michael F. Giangreco, Linda Davern, Doug Fisher, Bobbi Schnorr, and Alice Udvari-Solner.

We would like to extend deepest thanks to Kenna Colley, Christine Burton, Johnna Elliott, and Cynthia Pitonyak, who provided valuable contributions, including the case studies and many of the planning approaches and individualized adaptations described in this book. These outstanding educators have served at various times in roles including special education consulting teachers, administrators, in-service trainers, and technical assistance providers and have aided a number of school systems in enhancing their use of inclusive education practices.

To all the educators, parents, and students
who are working to create and maintain
inclusive school environments:
places where all students have membership,
enjoy social relationships with peers,
and have the needed supports to learn
what is important for them to be successful in life

Chapter 1

Inclusive Programming

The Big Picture

This book is designed to be a practical, hands-on resource for use by teams of general and special educators who share responsibility for educating elementary, middle, and high school students with and without disabilities in inclusive classrooms. The book has three main purposes: 1) to describe flexible, accommodating teaching practices that make the general education classroom suitable for students with a wide range of abilities and learning needs, 2) to provide a process for making decisions about modifying instructional activities for particular students when necessary, and 3) to give concrete examples of planning formats and instructional materials that have been developed by teachers to design and monitor modifications for individual students.

Most of the student-specific tools and strategies illustrated in this book were contributed by teachers in several school districts who have put inclusive education practices into action. Although these contributors are master teachers who have years of experience in inclusive practices and who have the support of their school and school-division administrators, they are nonetheless teachers who face the same challenges and demands as their colleagues around the country. These challenges include the demands for curriculum coverage and academic achievement that are so pressing for educators in today's era of high-stakes testing and public accountability systems. Therefore, even though the principles and approaches described in this book are presented as ideals, they come from real teachers in real classrooms. Some strategies have been adapted from the published work of other educators (e.g., Davern, Ford, Erwin, Schnorr, & Rogan, 1993; Ford et al., 1995; Giangreco, Cloninger, & Iverson, 1998; Jorgensen, 1998; Sailor, Gee, & Karasoff, 1993; Udvari-Solner, 1994; Villa & Thousand, 2000). Strategies continue to evolve as various teams of teachers working with various students apply these strategies creatively.

Although it takes great effort—on the part of many people across many years—to prepare a school system and its schools to provide effective inclusive education, the primary focus of this book is on classroom strategies rather than on the process of making school systems more inclusive. We do not extensively address the systemic change efforts that go into moving students from segregated or self-contained classrooms to integrated or inclusive classrooms. However, we do provide some helpful references (see Appendix B) and, in the final section of this chapter, suggest a general process, as well as some specific strategies, for moving forward with systems change efforts.

We also do not focus on the development of individualized education programs (IEPs), although we do provide some general information about IEPs for students in inclusive settings. The suggestions given about IEPs are consistent with the federal legislation contained in the Individuals with Disabilities Education Act (IDEA) Amendments of 1997 (PL 105-17), but readers should, of course, consult with their local and state specialists concerning informal norms and formal regulations to which they should adhere. References that detail the process of developing IEPs for inclusive programs are provided in Appendix B.

Instead, this book focuses on the processes of designing instruction that accommodates as wide a range of student learning characteristics as possible and making adaptations for individual students with IEPs. It is assumed that these students are starting the school year in an inclusive classroom with a classroom teacher who 1) considers the student to be a full member of the class, 2) has the support of a collaborating or consulting special education teacher, and 3) has the assistance of other support personnel as determined by the needs of the student.

This chapter provides an overview of some of the broad school and classroom practices that set the stage for effectively educating students in inclusive classes. Chapter 2 outlines a selection of the teaching practices that have been demonstrated to be effective in enhancing student achievement, particularly the achievement of students in mixed-ability classrooms. Chapter 3 provides a model for thinking about the process of making adaptations—the elements of curriculum and instruction that can be modified for individual students—and the criteria used to judge what makes a good adaptation. Chapter 4 illustrates the steps and procedures used to design and implement individualized adaptations and the monitoring and evaluation of those adaptations. Chapter 5 provides arrays of ideas for adapting instructional activities in basic skills (reading, writing, and math) and content areas, as well as a discussion of issues related to adapting tests and other assessments for individual students.

Throughout this book, each planning format or adaptation strategy is illustrated using case examples of students we have known. Blank copies of some of the forms used in these examples are provided in Appendix A. These case examples include students ages 5–22 who have a range of learning and support needs, such as

- Daniel, a first-grade student who has severe disabilities including cerebral palsy and mental retardation
- Melanie, a fourth grader who has autism
- Vanessa, a sixth-grade student with a learning disability
- Sam, a ninth-grade student who has a behavioral disorder and Asperger syndrome
- Walter, an eleventh grader who has mental retardation

SIX KEY ELEMENTS OF INCLUSIVE EDUCATION

Six key elements are required for the successful functioning of inclusive education (see Figure 1.1):

1. An inclusive program model
2. An inclusive culture in the school
3. Collaborative teaming and problem solving
4. Accommodation of curricular and instructional practices in the classroom
5. Strategies for making individualized adaptations
6. Strategies to facilitate peer relationships and supports

We provide specific strategies that could be used to improve each element of your school's inclusive practices. Most schools have some type of school improvement plan

---

1. *Inclusive program model:* Staffing arrangements, service delivery methods, and administrative support that enable students to receive appropriate services within inclusive, age-appropriate settings
2. *Inclusive culture in the school:* A vision of a diverse community that is put into practice
3. *Collaborative teaming and problem solving:* Skills and strategies used by general education and special education teachers for productive co-planning, communication, problem solving, and teaching
4. *Accommodation of curricular and instructional practices in the classroom:* Teaching that is known to be effective for all learners
5. *Strategies for making individualized adaptations:* Agreed-upon methods for planning, implementing, and evaluating the adaptations needed by individual students
6. *Strategies to facilitate peer relationships and supports:* Formal and informal ways to foster age-appropriate interactions and relationships among students with disabilities and their classmates

Figure 1.1. Six key elements of inclusive education.

or action plan that has been developed through a self-study process. An ideal approach to promoting and improving a school's inclusive practices is to incorporate goals and strategies related to the elements of inclusive education into the existing school improvement plan.

An Inclusive Program Model

In nearly every school district in the country, teachers, parents, and administrators are discussing issues related to the inclusion of students with disabilities in general education classrooms. People have come to use the terms *inclusive education* and *full inclusion* to describe a wide variety of special education programming options. In this book, we use these terms more narrowly. We define *inclusive education* or *full inclusion* as providing necessary services and supports for students with disabilities from within a homebase in general education classes in neighborhood schools.

According to the definition given in Figure 1.2, inclusive education means that individualized supports follow the student; therefore, students with disabilities are not isolated from their peers without disabilities. This definition also means that participation in general classes and other age-appropriate activities is the goal for all students. However, no absolute, across-the-board decisions are made

for all students; the IEP process is the means by which decisions are made regarding which of a student's needs are addressed inside or outside of the classroom. Such decisions are based on the skills to be taught and where instruction to address those skills is best delivered, not simply based on students' disability classifications. True inclusive education requires collaborative teaming to plan individual students' daily schedules and instruction and to incorporate special education services and supports into the ongoing classroom schedule. (Another way to describe this approach to service delivery is to say that the services are pulled in to the classroom.) It does *not* mean that students no longer receive specialized instruction and related services or that students are thrown into the mainstream to sink or swim. Indeed, the federal definition of *special education* is "specially designed instruction," a definition that makes no reference to the place where such instruction occurs.

Notice that inclusive education or full inclusion is different from the following types of programming:

• *Full integration:* Students with IEPs are based in general education classrooms, but all students do not necessarily have the opportunity to attend their neighborhood schools. Students may be clustered in designated schools according to their disability classifications.

✓ The opportunity for all students to attend the neighborhood schools they would attend if they did not have disabilities

✓ All students based in general education homerooms and classes

✓ General and special education teacher consultation and collaboration to incorporate special supports and services into age-appropriate school and community environments

✓ Flexible and individualized decision making about students' individualized education programs (including learning goals, services provided, and where and how instruction takes place) that is not solely based on disability categories

✓ All students learning what is important for them to learn, which may vary from one student to another

Figure 1.2. Definition of inclusive education.

- *Partial integration:* Students with IEPs receive a combination of pull-in and pull-out services. They tend to be integrated into general education classes for nonacademic portions of the school day. Students with IEPs do not necessarily attend their neighborhood schools but may be clustered in designated schools.

- *Student- or school-level inclusion:* Instead of a districtwide effort to provide inclusive opportunities for all students, particular students are provided with inclusive programming because of the efforts of their parents or particular schools have become inclusive due to the advocacy of faculty, parents, and/or administrators.

Creating a truly inclusive school can require many changes in aspects of school organization and structure that may at first glance seem far removed from the teaching and learning that goes on within the classroom. However, the ways students are assigned to schools, the ways students are assigned to teachers and classrooms, and the ways resources are allocated all have a significant impact on what happens among the teachers and students in a school. The effectiveness of inclusive education as a way to provide educational services depends on many variables in addition to teachers' knowledge and use of the most effective teaching methods.

An inclusive program model is a system by which appropriate special education services and supports are delivered to students who need them without removing those students from the schools and classrooms attended by their typical peers (see Figure 1.3). If students with disabilities in your school are not scheduled into general classes first and provided with special education supports and services within that setting before other alternatives are developed on an individual basis, then revising the program model is the place to start. An inclusive program model entails a number of features, including 1) methods for determining what services and supports students require in order to be successful in inclusive settings and 2) methods for getting those services and supports to the students. In other words, an inclusive program model requires appropriate staffing arrangements and appropriate service delivery methods.

What the Research Says

In the monograph *Inclusive Schooling Practices: Pedagogical and Research Foundations,* McGregor and Vogelsberg (1998) summarized the literature base on the best approaches to supporting students with disabilities in inclusive settings. The monograph gives the background and history of the inclusive schooling movement, provides descriptions of instructional practices that are effective for diverse students, and summarizes the research about inclusive education. Some of the key findings from the research: 1) students with disabilities demonstrate high levels of social interaction in inclusive settings, but physical presence alone does not guarantee positive social outcomes; 2) interactive, small-group contexts facilitate skill acquisition and social acceptance; 3) friendships do develop between students with disabilities and typical peers; 4) teachers play an important role in facilitating the development of friendships; 5) the performance of typically developing students is not compromised by the inclusion of students with disabilities; 6) parent support for inclusion is positively affected by actual experience; and 7) although many teachers are initially reluctant about inclusive education, support and experience make them more confident in their abilities. McGregor and Vogelsberg's monograph is useful to those who want advice about how to implement inclusive programs, and to those who want to be more knowledgeable about the research on the outcomes of inclusive schooling.

Figure 1.3. What we know about best practices in inclusive education.

Staffing Arrangements

Beside removing the previous physical separation between special and general education students, creating an inclusive program model means re-organizing the ways that students, teachers, and support staff are assigned to classrooms. In inclusive program models, students with IEPs are full and genuine members of the general education classroom but still have an IEP manager and/or consulting teacher who has specialized knowledge and competencies to ensure that the student receives appropriate education. The ease with which a school can assign reasonable student caseloads to special education teachers—and the ease with which those teachers can coordinate, plan, and deliver services to the students on their caseload—depends on a number of variables. One such variable is the state's special education teacher licensure categories. If teacher licensure or endorsement categories are based on discrete disability categories and a school deems that there are not enough students with a particular disability category in the school to warrant hiring a special education teacher who has credentials in that category, then the special education teachers in that school must have multiple categorical licensures.

The size of the general school population and the number of students who receive special education can present a variety of challenges. In a smaller school where there are few special education teachers, scheduling the special educators for pull-in services or collaborative teaching arrangements can be difficult. In addition, the population of students receiving special education is in constant flux: A staffing arrangement that was satisfactory in September may be disastrous by January, depending on the rate at which additional students are identified to receive special education and on the movement of students in and out of the school district or attendance zone. Listing these challenging variables is not to suggest that if a school faces some of these challenges, it will not be able to move forward in improving its inclusive programming. Instead, the point is that it is important to analyze the nature of the challenge being faced and not to assume that adapting the teaching methods and materials is the answer to every problem.

Inclusive schools use a variety of staffing arrangements, and those arrangements are seldom static from year to year. What those staffing arrangements have in common is that the administrators and teachers in the school have devised some strategy that enables each special education teacher to collaborate with a particular group of general education teachers. Three of the more frequently used inclusive staffing arrangements include

1. *Grade-level teams or families* (in elementary schools), in which a special education teacher provides direct and indirect services for most or all of the identified students at one or more particular grade levels. For example, in an elementary school with five special education teachers, one special educator might have a caseload comprising all of the kindergarten and first-grade students with IEPs, and the other four teachers would serve one grade each. In a smaller school, every special educator may be assigned to multiple grade levels, and in a very large school, multiple special educators may be assigned to each grade level. Because neither the number of students with IEPs at each grade level nor the overall number of students with IEPs in the school is static, the assignment of special education teachers to grade levels may also change as necessary during the school year, or at least annually.

2. *Interdepartmental teams, pods, or families* (in middle schools), in which a special education teacher serves all of the students with IEPs within one or more particular school team. This is in keeping with the typical middle-school staffing model, which clusters groups of students with interdepartmental or interdisciplinary groups of teachers.

3. *Departmental teams* (in high schools), in which special education teachers serve any and all identified students within the classes in particular subject areas (and, in larger high schools, within a particular grade level or levels). For example, of the 10 special education teachers at a high school, four might collaborate with the English Department, four with the Math Department, and two with the Science Department. In this staffing arrangement, the special education teachers would still have a caseload of students with IEPs but would not necessarily provide services for those same students throughout the day. Instead, special education teachers might provide support directly to students on their caseload during one academic class per day and would coordinate the remainder of the supports and services provided for the students across the day.

Notice that a hallmark of these inclusive staffing arrangements is to specify the students with IEPs within particular general education classrooms as the responsibility of a special education teacher. However, determining specifically how the special education services are provided for the students with IEPs in those classrooms is a different issue. In any of these staffing arrangements, the general educator and special educator may or may not actually teach particular lessons cooperatively. It is sometimes assumed that *collaborative teaming* between general and special educators is synonymous with *cooperative teaching*, but it is not. The specific ways and means by which the teachers on a collaborative team share the responsibility for teaching the students with IEPs in a particular classroom is determined by, among other things, the number of students on the special educator's caseload, the number of classrooms that the special educator supports, and, of course, the nature and extent of the support needs of those students. For example, in our inservice training and technical assistance work with school districts in Virginia and elsewhere, we have worked with schools that have student populations that vary widely in size, including metropolitan high schools that have 20 or more special education teachers and small, rural high schools that have one or two special education teachers. In one high school we know, two special education teachers, one working full time and one working half time, were responsible for 75 students with IEPs who were enrolled in virtually every class offered at the school. In that situation, there simply was very little chance for the special education teachers to engage in cooperative teaching with the general education teachers. At this particular school, the special educators and their colleagues decided to focus the special educators' co-teaching on the ninth-grade English classes, which seemed to be one of the most fundamental classes in the high school career of many students with IEPs, particularly those with learning disabilities.

It is important to note that the formula for determining pupil–teacher ratios does not automatically change when an inclusive program model is adopted. Inclusive programming does not necessarily require more staff resources, nor does it necessarily require less; it does require that staff resources be allocated differently.

Service Delivery Methods

The special education services and supports delivered in an inclusive program model also are different in some ways from the services delivered in pull-out or self-contained program models. In a pull-out resource or self-contained program model, most of a student's special education and related services are delivered directly to the student by special education teachers and related service providers (see Figure 1.4).

In an inclusive program model, services and supports may be delivered using a wider array of methods. Students' special education and related services, given in time per day or week on the free, appropriate public education (FAPE) section of every IEP, would include not only instruction delivered by a

What the Research Says

In some schools, special education teachers can only be found in special education resource rooms or in self-contained classes. Having students move back and forth between the resource room and the general education classroom all day means that the special education teacher:

- Does not know what is happening in the general education classroom and cannot provide support that is relevant
- Does not have a feel for how students generalize their skills from the resource room into the general education classroom
- Is not familiar with students' behavior in the general education classroom
- Cannot support students in the general education classroom or monitor support given by paraprofessionals

The same problem exists when a teacher remains in a self-contained class all day to support some students who are not ready to participate in the general education classroom. Solutions for these problems lie in having an inclusive program model that operates in the school so that no teacher or student is self-contained, and all special education teachers have schedules that allow daily and predictable movement into general education classrooms containing their students. Teaching assistants benefit from having individualized job descriptions that delineate their team roles and responsibilities (see also Figure 1.10).

Figure 1.4.   Where the special education teacher is.

special education teacher and related services delivered by therapists or other specialists but also consultation between and among the teachers and other service providers and the support of instructional assistants or paraprofessionals (see Figure 1.5). These direct services might be provided on a pull-in or pull-out basis, depending on a number of variables, and might include a variety of activities in addition to direct student instruction. The services provided in inclusive settings may include the following:

- *Consultation,* an indirect service, which may be provided by a special educator to the general education teacher or may occur between or among specialists. Consultation may include co-planning, providing information, conducting peer planning and problem-solving sessions, developing or adapting materials, collecting and analyzing data, developing and monitoring behavior support plans, and doing demonstrations or coaching.

- *Instruction,* a direct service, which may be delivered one-to-one, in a small group of students, or via cooperative teaching to a large group

- *Instructional support,* a direct service, which might include providing individualized cues and prompts during a classroom lesson, providing physical assistance with functional routines, and monitoring transitions. Instructional support can be delivered by a special education teacher or by an assistant.

For example, Daniel, a first grader who has multiple disabilities, receives services by each on these delivery methods. Daniel's special education and related services are listed in the FAPE section of his IEP, as shown in Table 1.1. Notice that in order for Daniel and many other students with disabilities to receive their special education and related services within inclusive settings, those settings must be accessible. All areas of the classroom and the school must be accessible to students who use

What the Research Says

In addition to the changes that inclusive programming requires for teachers' roles, it requires reshaping roles for paraprofessionals (also known as paraeducators and instructional assistants). Because special education teachers plan and coordinate—but do not directly deliver—all special education services to students in inclusive classrooms, paraprofessionals are increasingly being assigned to provide assistance with students' physical needs, deliver certain types of instruction, and provide other sorts of supports to students, especially those who have severe and multiple disabilities. Research has raised concerns regarding the effects of the increasing use of paraprofessionals in inclusive education programs on:

- The occurrence of peer interactions and the development of peer relationships (Giangreco, Edelman, Luiselli, & MacFarland, 1997)
- The classroom teacher's engagement with the student (Giangreco, Broer, & Edelman, 2001)
- The student's development of skills for independence (Downing, Ryndak, & Clark, 2000)

It is important to ensure that paraprofessionals have clearly defined and appropriate job responsibilities, adequate training, and effective supervision. Among the solutions suggested by these researchers, and other experts who have critically examined the use of paraprofessionals in educational programs for students with severe disabilities (Brown, Farrington, Knight, Ross, & Ziegler, 1999; Giangreco & Doyle, 2002; Mueller & Murphy, 2001), are the following:

1. Provide each paraprofessional with an individualized job description that specifies the array of tasks to be done, which students he or she supports, and who the supervisor is.

2. Provide each paraprofessional with inservice training in providing support and instruction in ways that promote independence and do not inhibit peer interaction.

3. Use an objective decision-making model to determine the specific activities for which the student needs the assistance of a paraprofessional, and have a plan in place for reducing that support over time by encouraging independence and increasing the use of natural supports, including peers.

4. Special education teachers must develop written program plans and ensure that the paraprofessional receives modeling and coaching in how to deliver instruction and monitor progress by collecting student performance data. Special education teachers must also collect student performance data themselves.

Figure 1.5.   The role of paraprofessionals in inclusive classrooms.

wheelchairs and other mobility-enhancing devices. Access to appropriate instructional materials, assistive technology, and nonacademic activities is also part of the equation when considering the supports and services required for inclusive classrooms.

An Inclusive Culture in the School

Books and journal articles on inclusive education suggest that one fundamental aspect of schools that seek to promote inclusion of all students is a school culture that is anchored in a sense of community and emphasizes the value of human diversity (e.g., Fisher, Sax, & Pumpian, 1999; Jorgensen, 1998; Salisbury, Palombaro, & Hollowood, 1993; Solomon, Schaps, Watson, & Battistich, 1992; Van Dyke, Pitonyak, & Gilley, 1996; Villa & Thousand, 2000). Inclusive schools are welcoming and accommodating for *all* students. The professional literature on effective schools and school improvement emphasizes themes that are remarkably consistent with the professional literature devoted specifically to creating effective, inclusive schools. For example, to a great extent, effective schools welcome and capitalize on diversity. Effective schools tend to have a collaborative culture

Table 1.1.   Daniel's special education and related services

Services	Frequency	Location
Special education instruction for language arts (co-teaching)	1 hour per day	First-grade classroom
Special education consultation for co-planning, preparation of adapted materials, data collection, and demonstrations	30 minutes per day	First-grade classroom
Special education aide support for math, arrival, lunch, departure, and bathroom routines	4 hours per day	First-grade classroom, cafeteria, restroom, hallways
Occupational therapy	20 minutes per week	First-grade classroom
Physical therapy	20 minutes per week	First-grade classroom
Pull-in direct services	20 minutes per week	First-grade classroom
Pull-out evaluation of movement and equipment	20 minutes once every 6 weeks	Special education office
Speech-language therapy (direct service, within small-group activities)	20 minutes per week	First-grade classroom

and a strong sense of community (see Figure 1.6). The collaboration among teachers, parents, administrators, and other community members in these schools goes beyond merely getting along with one another to making deliberate efforts to work jointly toward creating a school that reflects goals and values that are important to the community (Good & Brophy, 1986; Marzano, 2000).

Creating a shared vision and a shared sense of values in a school is not easy to accomplish—or even to describe. However, there is little doubt that inclusive schools are based in a commitment to the value of community and equality. They have a warm, caring culture that emphasizes acceptance of all students, is based in a sense of community and social connectedness, and emphasizes

Voices from the Classroom

Both Kenna Colley and Cyndi Pitonyak have been special education consulting teachers at an elementary school where the principal has successfully created a strong sense of belonging for students, teachers, and parents. Kenna and Cyndi note that this principal attends to the "big picture" and also does little things that count toward making each member of the school community feel valued. Some of the things the principal has done to make people feel noticed and appreciated include the following:

- Bringing food to faculty meetings—the principal provides snacks the first month, then the teachers at each grade level sign up for subsequent months
- Setting a monthly lunch date with parents
- Swapping roles with teachers
- Being part of students' behavior support plans by, for example, regularly visiting a classroom to encourage a particular student
- Acting as a substitute teacher so that teachers have more time to meet
- Getting release time for teachers and instructional assistants to attend inservices
- Putting notes of appreciation and recognition in faculty and staff mailboxes

Figure 1.6.   How one principal builds community.

- A variety of schoolwide and individual classroom activities to demonstrate how to value different characteristics and abilities, such as families' sharing cultural information in the school or community and having a community fair to end a thematic unit on the customs and contributions of various cultural and ethnic groups
- Organized activities to welcome newcomers, including both students and their families and new faculty and staff members
- Open houses, musical and artistic activities, and other opportunities for students, staff, and parents to meet
- Community-helping activities, such as providing food or services for those in need, organizing recycling and clean-up campaigns, and working in a community garden or park
- Cross-age peer tutoring programs, peer support networks, class meetings, and democratic problem-solving sessions
- Disability and ability awareness activities, such as surveying and improving the accessibility of the building and classrooms

Figure 1.7. Activities to help create a caring, inclusive school community culture.

the development of self-direction and concern for others. This culture does not simply come about automatically as a result of a feeling of caring; instead, there are active efforts to put the values of community and equality into practice (see Figure 1.7).

If there is concern that your school does not have a culture that could be described as inclusive, improvement can begin with holding open discussions (e.g., at faculty meetings, parent–teacher organization meetings, grade-level open houses for parents) about questions such as these:

- Is diversity valued in this school? Are there individuals or groups who do not feel truly welcome or do not believe they have genuine input?

- Are we a community? Do we share certain fundamental values about why we are here and how we should treat one another?

- Do we expect excellence and equity for all students? What are some specific ways in which we demonstrate this value?

An additional strategy that can assist in developing a more inclusive school culture is to provide all teachers and other staff members in the school with adequate information about the rationale for an inclusive approach to education. Research has shown that when

embarking on school change efforts, participants in the change process want these questions answered first: Why are we doing this? What are the benefits? (Janney, Snell, Beers, & Raynes, 1995). Figure 1.8 provides brief summaries of several ways to explain the rationale and benefits of inclusive education. Again, this strategy might be undertaken initially by the inclusion committee and then expanded to include the entire faculty, staff, and school community.

Collaborative Teaming and Problem Solving

In the United States, federal special education law has always required teaming as part of the IEP process, as outlined in the IDEA Amendments of 1997 (PL 105-17). However, inclusive education tends to require even more ongoing communication and collaboration than other program models. In an inclusive program, the IEP team may function much as it has in the past. But inclusive programming requires special and general education teachers and support staff to share responsibility for educating students on a daily basis. This means that teachers' roles must be defined in new ways because one teacher alone is no longer responsible for a classroom of students. It requires that general and spe-

- *Civil rights:* Segregation based on disability is inherently unequal and unconstitutional (*Mills v. Board of Education of the District of Columbia,* 1972; *Pennsylvania Association for Retarded Children v. Commonwealth of Pennsylvania,* 1972).

- *Social benefits:* Students without disabilities learn to accept and value differences (Helmstetter, Peck, & Giangreco, 1994; Peck, Carlson, & Helmstetter, 1992; Staub & Peck, 1994–1995). Students with disabilities obtain social and emotional benefits (Baker, Wang, & Wahlberg, 1994–1995; Fisher & Meyer, 2002; Fryxell & Kennedy, 1995; Kennedy, Shukla, & Fryxell, 1997; Lipsky & Gartner, 1995; Vaughn, Elbaum, Schumm, & Hughes, 1998).

- *Educational benefits:* Skill acquisition by students with disabilities is enhanced (Baker, Wang, & Wahlberg, 1994–1995; Hundert, Mahoney, Mundy, & Vernon, 1998; Hunt, Ferron-Davis, Beckstead, Curtsin, & Goetz, 1994; Hunt, Staub, Alwell, & Goetz,1994; Lipsky & Gartner, 1995). Achievement of students without disabilities is not impaired (Dugan et al., 1995; Hunt, Staub, Alwell, & Goetz, 1994; Staub & Peck, 1994–1995).

- *Psychological benefits:* Humans need safety and acceptance in order to have motivation to achieve; students with disabilities cannot achieve without acceptance (Kunc, 1992).

- *Administrative benefits:* Having two separate systems—special education and general education—is irrational and inefficient (Lipsky & Gartner, 1997; Skrtic, 1991).

- *Legal benefits:* Students should not be removed from the school and classroom they would attend if they did not have a disability "unless they have not been successful there, even with the addition of supplementary aids and services" (Least restrictive environment [LRE] clause of Individuals with Disabilities Education Act [IDEA] Amendments of 1997 [PL 105-17]).

Figure 1.8.   Rationale for inclusive education.

cial education teachers work together in a variety of collaborative teams. These team models include student-centered support teams, grade-level teams, families or houses, and departmental teams.

Inclusive education also requires that team members have the needed skills to communicate, plan, and deliver services jointly. Of course, the need for joint planning time must be considered as an integral part of the design of an inclusive program model. The problems of finding joint planning time have no easy solutions. One possible answer is to reduce the amount of time needed for planning individualized adaptations. This can be accomplished in several ways, including 1) viewing initial planning as planning for the entire class, not as planning for typical learners that will be followed by subsequent planning for every student with an IEP; 2) learning skills for effective teaming and problem solving, so that the time you do spend together is focused and productive; and 3) using specific, agreed-upon formats for planning, including forms for documenting the deci-

sions made about students' adaptations, and ways of communicating between meetings. The preparation, planning, and skill development that must be done to enable teachers, parents, and other service providers to work together effectively as a team are addressed thoroughly in *Collaborative Teaming* (Snell & Janney, 2004), another volume in the *Teachers' Guides to Inclusive Practices* series.

One initial step toward improving your teaming efforts is to adopt or develop strategies for defining and clarifying team members' roles and responsibilities. The Team Roles and Responsibilities Checklist offers a structure for generating discussion of questions about the responsibilities of each team member, as well as a reminder of some of the issues about classroom roles, rules, and routines that should be discussed by any team of special and general educators who share responsibility for students in the same classroom. The Team Roles and Responsibilities Checklist should be completed early in the school year, although it is a good idea to revisit the checklist at the end of each grading period or semester to be sure that agreed upon roles and responsibilities are being fulfilled.

This checklist could be completed separately for each classroom team or by a larger team such as a grade-level team, depending on how much collaborative teaming occurs among the general education teachers with whom one special education teacher is associated. For example, in one elementary school, the fifth-grade classroom teachers' teaming is very strong: They cooperatively plan thematic units, share materials, and do frequent cross-grouping of their students. The special education teacher who supports all IEP students in the fifth grade is an active member of the fifth-grade team and engages in grade-level planning with them. At the beginning of the school year, the entire fifth-grade team, along with the relevant specialists and support personnel, jointly discussed the Team Roles and Responsibilities Checklist and decided to adopt essentially the same configuration of roles and responsibilities for the adults in all of the fifth-grade classrooms. However, in other situations, particularly at the high school level, teams may find that each classroom team needs to complete the checklist separately.

Figure 1.9 shows how staff roles and responsibilities were divided for a fourth-grade classroom team in a fully inclusive school. The completed checklist makes it evident that Ms. Ramirez, the fourth-grade teacher, intended for the students with disabilities to be grouped with the class. Note, for example, that Ms. Ramirez took responsibility for arranging IEP conferences, just as she took responsibility for arranging parent conferences for other students in the class. The special education teacher, Ms. Pitonyak, remained the IEP manager for all students receiving special education in the class and retained primary responsibility for the legalities and paperwork associated with the IEPs. However, Ms. Ramirez was responsible for ongoing communication with parents of all students in her class.

It is important that members of any collaborative team discuss the values and standards that will guide their work. Difficulties in team functioning can result from a lack of skills in teaming and from a lack of shared values for making decisions and evaluating student success. Sometimes, it is clear from the start that team members do not share the same beliefs about the value of inclusive education in general or the value of a particular student's being able to participate socially and instructionally in activities with her or his classmates. Often, discussions among team members about what they *do* value may help the team to agree about key practices that will guide their shared work. For example, the team may be able to agree on the value of hands-on lessons or a language-rich classroom or on the importance of in-class support during reading instruction for students who are struggling with their reading. If each team member will make some compromises in order to reach agreement about the common practices that are valued by the team, there is a starting point for collaboration and the development of additional shared values.

In a very practical way, a collaborative team needs certain agreed-upon values because those values will be the standards for evaluating classroom adaptations and student success. Although teams typically make unspoken assumptions about team or individual values, *open discussion* of beliefs and values can enhance team effectiveness. For example, in Chapter 3, we describe two criteria that should be met by the individualized adaptations that are designed for students: Adaptations should enable instructional and social participation and be only as special as necessary. These criteria are based on a number of assumptions about teaching, learning, and what it means to be included in a classroom community. As a team creates and adapts planning formats and systems of adaptations for individual students, team members should explicitly discuss the criteria that they will use to select adaptations and evaluate the results for students. Discussion of these two principles at a grade-level or student-focused team meeting might prove to be a step toward a greater sense of shared values by the team in question.

Team Roles and Responsibilities Checklist

Classroom   _Ramirez/4th_   **Date**   _10/24/04_

Teaching and Support Team Members:

Ramirez   Classroom teacher   _O'Donnell_   Instructional assistant

Pitonyak   Special education teacher   _____   Other

x = Primary responsibility
input = Input into decision making and/or implementation

Roles and responsibilities	Who is responsible?			
	Classroom teacher	Special education teacher	Instructional assistant	Other: _____
Developing lessons/units	x	x		
Adapting curriculum	input	x		
Adapting teaching methods	x	x	input	
Adapting materials	input	x	input	
Monitoring weekly/daily student progress	x	x (reports, IEP)	x (data log)	
Assigning grades	x	x		
Assigning duties to/supervising assistants	x (daily)	x (training)		
Scheduling team meetings a. IEP teams b. Core planning teams (specific students)	x input	input x		
Daily/weekly communication with parents	x	input	input	
Communication/collaboration with related services		x (service coordinator)	input (notes, logs)	
Facilitating peer relationships and supports	x	x (peer planning)	input	

Figure 1.9.   Team Roles and Responsibilities Checklist. (From Ford, A., Messenheimer-Young, T., Toshner, J., Fitzgerald, M.A., Dyer, C., Glodoski, J., & Laveck, J. [1995, July]. *A team planning packet for inclusive education.* Milwaukee: Wisconsin School Inclusion Project; adapted by permission.)

Accommodation of Curricular and Instructional Practices in the Classroom

Just as an inclusive school culture is socially accommodating for all students, effective teaching practices in the classroom tend to accommodate a wide range of students.

Many students, including students with and without disabilities, are not likely to be successful in traditional classrooms with a "one size fits all" approach to teaching and learning. *Unaccommodating teaching* relies heavily on a textbook-based curriculum in which every student is expected to be on the same page at the same time, to read aloud over and over again, and to answer questions at the end of each chapter. Large-group lectures followed by uniform seatwork exercises also are ineffective for many learners, if used as the primary means of instruction.

Accommodating teaching refers to the use of curriculum approaches and instructional strategies that are effective in enhancing achievement for most students. From the perspective of special education, one exciting thing about the growing emphasis on the use of research-based or evidence-based teaching practices is that such practices tend to be precisely those that are effective for most learners, regardless of disability (e.g., Marzano, 2003; National Reading Panel, n.d.). Classrooms that accommodate a wide range of students are characterized by a climate of warmth and inclusiveness and by curricular and instructional practices that emphasize choice, meaning, active learning, and student interaction. Other terms that might be applied to this type of curriculum and instruction are *learner-centered, process-oriented,* and *communication-based* (Udvari-Solner & Thousand, 1996). Teachers in these classrooms utilize flexible, fluid student groupings and multiple approaches to content delivery and student products. However, this is not an overly permissive approach to instruction. Lessons are carefully structured so that new information is tied to students' existing knowledge, instructions are clear, models and demonstrations are provided, and students engage in repeated opportunities to

practice using new skills and knowledge with increasing independence and generalization. Students learn to make choices and decisions and to be active rather than passive learners. To the extent that we promote and incorporate accommodating curricular and instructional practices, we also are helping to create classrooms where more children with *and* without disabilities can be successful.

In Chapter 2, we give fuller descriptions of some of these accommodating teaching practices. The resource list in Appendix B gives complete reference citations for the resources that served as the sources for these descriptions; consult them for more information. We would not want to wait until all schools and classrooms are accommodating before providing students with IEPs with access to general education. However, in a sense, the use of evidence-based teaching practices makes a sound prerequisite to the development of any adaptations for individual students. Indeed, the use of such practices actually makes the task of developing adaptations for individual students easier. In one sense, the least intrusive and most inclusive adaptation is made when teachers adapt their teaching strategies for the entire class. As represented graphically by Figure 1.10, the more inclusive the school culture and the more accommodating the classroom, the fewer individualized adaptations are required.

Strategies for Making Individualized Adaptations

This key to inclusive education—having specific, agreed-upon strategies for making individualized adaptations for students—is one of the primary topics of this book. One assumption behind our approach to inclusive education is that neither physical presence nor being present only for socialization is an adequate goal. Students with IEPs can and should meet their individual educational goals in inclusive settings, even when their educational goals are somewhat or very different from the goals of their classmates who do not have IEPs.

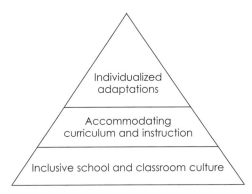

Figure 1.10. Accommodating schools and classrooms reduce the need for individualized adaptations.

In order for students with more extensive disabilities to meet critical learning goals, the teams of adults who are working together in inclusive classrooms must explicitly identify the processes they will use for making joint decisions about individualized modifications and supports and for communicating decisions among all team members. Chapter 4 offers many planning and communication strategies to use or adapt.

Because inclusive education requires individualization, it is important for teams to take a problem-solving orientation toward their work. Although resources such as this one can help by providing guidelines and ideas for educating students in inclusive ways, the many differences among children, communities, and classrooms require that teams view their work as an ongoing process of figuring out what works for a particular student in a particular classroom situation. We cannot emphasize too strongly that inclusive education is an evolutionary process. The question to ask is: How can we make it work in this school for these students? The answer requires the use of a problem-solving process, not a list or menu of adaptations developed by others. The model for making adaptations that is described in Chapter 3 and the steps in making adaptations for individual students that are illustrated in Chapter 4 provide a framework that can guide this decision-making and problem-solving process.

Strategies to Facilitate Peer Relationships and Supports

The sixth essential element of inclusive education is the facilitation of support networks and other positive relationships among students. Although ample evidence shows that friendships and a variety of other social interactions occur between students with disabilities and their classmates in inclusive classrooms, simply placing students with disabilities in an inclusive classroom does not guarantee the development of positive social relationships (McGregor & Vogelsberg, 1998). Without direct and indirect facilitation

of social relationships and peer support, students with disabilities may experience only partial inclusion in the social life of the classroom and school (Deshler et al., 2002).

Strategies for promoting the development of peer supports and constructive relationships among classmates with and without disabilities are addressed in depth in *Social Relationships and Peer Support* (Snell & Janney, 2000), another of the books in this series. Briefly, these strategies range from indirect approaches to improving the social environment and staff and student attitudes toward disability to directly building positive relationships between students. Indirectly influencing peer relationships by improving the social environment can occur by 1) providing students and staff with information and possibly simulations to increase understanding and appreciation of disabilities; 2) incidental (and sometimes explicit) modeling of appropriate ways to assist, relate to, and interact with students who have disabilities; and 3) modeling and even teaching explicit lessons on the use of respectful, person-first language, which refers to a disability as what a person has, not what a person is (Snell & Janney, 2000; Snow, 2004).

A variety of direct approaches to building peer relationships and support have been developed and tested in inclusive schools. These strategies include more structured group support processes, such as the McGill action planning system (MAPS; Vandercook, York, & Forest, 1989), making action plans (Forest & Lusthaus, 1989), personal futures planning (Mount & Zwernick, 1988), and person-centered planning (Browder, Bambara, & Belifore, 1997; Holburn & Vietze, 2002; Kincaid, 1996), and other, less structured peer support and problem-solving groups. All of these approaches involve goal setting and problem solving about ways to assist a student with a disability to become a full member of the social community. MAPS and personal futures planning invite peers to participate in planning and problem solving about the needs of a classmate with a disability. Teachers in inclusive classrooms often use adapted versions of such processes to do peer planning or peer problem solving for all students in the class, rather than only for the students with identified disabilities. Cooperative learning approaches that emphasize teaching students the social skills needed for effective teaming also have been used to promote equitable student interactions and relationships (Putnam, 1993; Thousand, Villa, & Nevin, 1994).

It is important, however, to be sensitive to the possible drawbacks of placing too much focus on peer helping relationships. Students with disabilities need purely social relationships with their peers and to be helpers to others, rather than always being the ones who are being helped. "We must be careful not to overemphasize the helper–helpee aspect of a relationship. Unless help is reciprocal, the inherent inequality between helper and helpee will contaminate the authenticity of the relationship. Friendship is not the same as help" (Van der Klift & Kunc, 1994, p. 393).

IMPROVING YOUR SCHOOL'S INCLUSIVE PRACTICES

Developing an effective inclusive education program is a process that requires attention to many elements besides those that directly involve teaching methods and materials. Like any large-scale, significant educational change effort, it requires a focused, systematic effort among administrators, general and special education teachers, parents, and support personnel. The teachers involved certainly may need professional development to increase their skills in the collaborative planning and delivery of instruction for diverse groups of students. However, many other variables—including the attitudes of the individuals involved, the culture of the school, the history of change efforts in the school district, and the existing program model—can inhibit or facilitate the use of the preferred instructional practices.

Evaluating Your School's Inclusive Practices

The Team Survey of Inclusive Practices can be used to assist in developing action plans for improving the inclusive programming in a particular school. (A blank form is provided on p. 124 of Appendix A). The survey addresses the six elements that have been described in this chapter as important keys to the process of putting an inclusive philosophy into action (see Table 1.2). Although the planning for individualized adaptations that is the main subject of this book is done by the core team that provides services for a student or students on a daily basis, this broad checklist might be completed by a grade-level team, a classroom team, or a planning group or inclusion committee that represents the entire building. The literature on school change virtually unanimously advocates the formation of a representative planning team, task force, or committee to guide the school through any significant change (e.g., Fashola & Slavin, 1998; Horsley & Kaser, 1999; McChesney, 1998; Quellmalz, Shields, & Knapp, 1995; Shields & Knapp, 1997). Whether this group is formed by a small group of teachers and parents who are interested in improving the inclusive practices in their classrooms or by a large-scale, systemwide effort to provide students with inclusive opportunities, the same principle applies. A significant change effort requires, among other things, a systematic planning effort by a group that represents the stakeholders who will be affected by the change.

The process of surveying and evaluating a particular school's inclusive practices involves several steps. Before completing the Team Survey of Inclusive Practices, the planning team should be sure that its members have some background information about the current state of affairs in the school and some knowledge of what constitutes an effective inclusive program. (Having all team members read and discuss this chapter might be one place to start.)

Completing the survey requires making judgments about the extent to which each of the six key elements for inclusive education is in place in the school. The rating scale is "1—We have not done it," "2—We have tried, but it needs improvement," and "3—We have done it well." At a team meeting, team members should discuss and then reach consensus on the rating for the six elements

Table 1.2. Key elements in effective schoolwide change initiatives

Elements	Strategies
Vision and values There is a clear vision of what the change entails and the rationale for change is clear. The focus of the change is on effective teaching and creating challenging learning experiences for all students.	Structure opportunities for teachers and parents to express ideas and values regarding the vision. Solicit input from teachers and parents to articulate a vision statement and value base. Adjust policies and procedures to reflect vision and values.
Collaborative teamwork Change leaders and representatives of stakeholder groups lead the change process by providing the faculty and community with a strong vision and an organizing framework for accomplishing the change. The school has strong collaboration and partnerships among teachers, families, and students.	Establish building-wide planning and problem-solving teams. Brainstorm creative strategies to provide time and opportunities for collaborative planning of instruction. Provide staff development on collaborative skills, including teamwork, problem solving, and effective meeting skills. Adopt a process for clearly defining team roles and responsibilities. Hold regular team meetings around individual students with agendas, assigned roles, and time limits. Implement ongoing home–school communication.
Involvement and commitment Each person who will be affected by the initiative is committed to achieving the vision.	Identify barriers and involve the people who will be affected by the change in addressing the barriers. Provide orientation activities for faculty, staff, parents, and community members. Listen to them, and find ways to collaboratively engage them in the change, including involving them in addressing barriers. Develop a school culture that nurtures staff collaboration and participation in decision making. Engage in advocacy and public relations.
Resources The infrastructure provides resources that support the change.	Create awareness of the way that the change affects other aspects of the school and community, including the interface between this change and other change initiatives. Align resources comprehensively.
Action plan A written plan is developed to guide and track the change.	Include measurable goals for the systems change team in the action plan or implementation plan. Incorporate best practice research into the plan. Make sure that student performance data are simple, collected often, and made visible. Use continuous evaluation to update and improve the plan. Map out a reasonable time frame for implementing the plan. (Longer is better.)
Professional development Faculty and staff have meaningful opportunities for professional development so that they can build the skills needed to implement the change.	Assess staff development needs. Provide opportunities for professional development, visitations, and sharing successes. Work with local universities and technical assistance programs to provide training. Incorporate topics, such as curriculum adaptation, behavioral support, and collaboration, into the school inservice plan.

Sources: Fashola & Slavin, 1998; Horsley & Kaser, 1999; Keenan, 1997; McChesney, 1998; Quellmalz, Shields, & Knapp, 1995; Schmoker, 1999; Shields, & Knapp, 1997; Van Dyke, Pitonyak, & Gilley, 1996; Voorhees, Landon, & Harvey, 1997

on the survey. If need for improvement is indicated for one or more elements, the planning team should then identify which of these elements should be action priorities at the present time. In the column headed "Action Priority," the team should assign a "high" to those elements that it wants to focus its efforts on right away and a "low" to those elements that can wait. One strategy for selecting action priorities is to begin with an element on which the team feels confident that it can have some impact. Another strategy is to set a goal, such as reaching a "2—We have tried but it needs improvement" on all six elements.

Steps and Strategies for Change

After assessing the school's current inclusive practices and selecting action priorities, the team should develop an action plan. Figure 1.11 presents a simple problem-solving format that is useful for educational team members who want to work together to improve the inclusive practices in their school. The problem-solving format, known as the Issue–

Action Plan, is one that is used by many of the teachers who contributed to this book. Issue–action planning helps the team to focus on specific issues that need solving and the steps that will be taken to address them.

The next step is to identify the issues, problems, challenges, or difficulties that stand in the way of obtaining a rating of "3—We have done it well" for each action priority identified on the Team Survey of Inclusive Practices. Then, the planning team should brainstorm about actions that could be taken to move toward improving or resolving each identified issue. Be as specific and concrete as possible. For example, "Develop and circulate to classroom teachers a one-page Program-at-a-Glance for each student with an IEP" is a specific, observable action. In contrast, "Improve communication about the needs of students with IEPs" is not a specific, observable action. After brainstorming, evaluate the possible actions that were generated, and decide which ones are both feasible and consistent with the goals and values of inclusive education. After deciding which actions you will take, then designate a timeline for

---

Student/Team _____ *5th Grade* _____ **Date** _____ *12/3/04* _____

Team Members Present _____ *Kenna, Maryanne (facilitator), Ginni, Tim, Sandy* _____

RE: ___ *Item #2 from "Team Survey of Inclusive Practices": Do we use collaborative team*

*planning and problem-solving strategies?* _____

Issue	Planned action	Who is responsible?
1. We spend too much meeting time on field trips, standardized testing, and so on, instead of coplanning class activities and individualized adaptations.	1. Do a written agenda at each meeting: Reserve the first half for individual student planning and the second half for organizational issues. Find or make agenda forms and make copies.	1. **Kenna**: Make/find agenda form; bring copies to meetings. **Everyone**: Take turns creating agenda and facilitating meetings.
2. We do not always follow through with the adaptation strategies we establish at meetings.	2. Spend first few minutes of each meeting reviewing and reporting on action items from last meeting.	2. **Maryanne**: Review action items. **Everyone**: Report on actions taken.

Figure 1.11. Issue–Action Plan.

the action and a person or people who will be responsible for taking the action.

The planning team should meet on a regular basis (at least once per month) to report on actions that have been taken, evaluate progress, and decide on next steps. The planning team also should agree to revisit the Team Survey of Inclusive Practices for a postaction evaluation of the six key elements. (One semester might be an appropriate amount of time.) At that time, the team can reevaluate the elements, using the second "Status" and "Action Priority" columns of the Team Survey of Inclusive Practices to record its ratings and can then compare total scores for the first and second ratings.

For example, the schoolwide inclusion committee that completed the Issue–Action Plan in Figure 1.11 had rated itself as a "2— We have tried, but it needs improvement" on item number two of the Team Survey of Inclusive Practices, the use of collaborative team planning and problem-solving strategies. Two team members had noticed that many of their core team meetings—meetings that were held to plan lesson adaptations for individual students—were being spent discussing upcoming field trips and the state-mandated standardized testing program. Another issue centered on team members' failing to implement some of the adaptation strategies that had been developed at meetings of the core team. The inclusion committee then brainstormed ways to collaborate more effectively and to increase individual accountability for implementing team decisions. They evaluated the ideas to determine which were the most feasible and consistent with their goal of creating truly inclusive classrooms. The team decided to 1) establish a written agenda at the beginning of each team meeting, 2) list first on the agenda reports on action responsibilities that had been accomplished since the last meeting, and 3) reserve the first half of each meeting for individual student planning before addressing administrative and organizational issues. Then, the team designated a timeline for each action and a person or people who would be responsible for achieving it.

For example, one team member volunteered to find or create an agenda form and to be responsible for gathering agenda items and recording them on the form. Another team member offered to record decisions, responsibilities, and timelines on the Issue–Action Plan form and to copy and distribute the forms to the rest of the team after each meeting. Figure 1.12 provides an example of the way in which another school conducted its inclusion committee meeting.

We urge you to take advantage of what other schools and school systems have learned about creating inclusive environments by examining some of the systems change steps, strategies, and resources provided in Table 1.2. It is not just a clever evasion to say that solving a problem is much easier when the problem has been correctly identified. Focusing improvement efforts on the right problem is one key to successful systems change efforts. For example, if a school is attempting to move toward more inclusive programming by maintaining pull-out resource room programs for students with certain disability labels (e.g., those with severe or multiple disabilities) or for certain subject areas (e.g., math, English), while also providing special education pull-in support for other students with IEPs, then the problems that teachers face stem from trying to operate two program models at the same time as much as they stem from the actual challenge of designing instructional activities that are suitable for students with and without disabilities. In a situation such as this, providing teachers with an inservice workshop on cooperative teaching will not solve the problem of how to get the teachers into the classroom at the same time so that they can teach together. The program model is the real problem in this instance, although it may well be true that the teachers would appreciate the opportunity to improve their skills in collaborative teaching and teaming.

We also cannot emphasize strongly enough the importance of viewing the road to inclusive education as a journey. Remember: You cannot go from point A to point B without

Voices from the Classroom

Kenna Colley, formerly a special education consulting teacher and now co-director of a special education training and technical assistance center, helped to establish an Inclusion Committee at her elementary school to aid the principal and teachers in identifying and addressing issues related to supporting teachers and students in inclusive classrooms. The students considered were not only those with IEPs but also students with limited English proficiency, struggling readers, and students with behavioral issues. The committee meetings were held on the first Monday of every month and were open to anyone who wanted to attend. At the beginning of each meeting, the group would count the number of people present and divide that number into 60 minutes—the time limit for the meetings—to determine how much time each person would be allotted on the agenda. Participants had to agree to come to the meeting prepared to present an issue by telling exactly what they needed. After each issue was presented, the group engaged in problem solving. If the issue was related to needed equipment, resources, or staff time, someone would agree to discuss the issue with the appropriate administrator. If the issue was teacher-related, the group's goal was to give that teacher five or six ideas with which to leave the meeting. The Inclusion Committee is no longer in operation because the issues that it addressed were so clearly general school issues (e.g., how do we meet the needs of students with reading difficulties?) rather than issues that were specific to the inclusion of students with disabilities at the school (e.g., how do we meet the needs of students with IEPs who have reading difficulties?). The Inclusion Committee eventually became part of the Continuous School Improvement Team.

Figure 1.12.   The Inclusion Committee.

taking the first step, the second step, and many, many subsequent steps along the way. Do not forget to celebrate your successes.

Another lesson that has been learned over and over again from the research on education change is that change requires each individual who is implementing the change to develop a new map of what his or her job is about. Teachers, as practitioners who care deeply about students' success, can gain motivation for a new program by seeing positive results for children. Starting small, with a pilot program that targets the provision of pull-in services and supports for all students in a particular grade level or for particular subjects areas or departments, can be an effective strategy to generate momentum for change.

SUMMARY

In this chapter, we introduced six elements that are essential to making inclusive class-rooms a reality. These key elements include a program model that is based on the belief that all students should be part of shared learning communities and a school culture that welcomes all sorts of diversity. Also essential are collaborative teaming practices that effectively support students and teachers, curricular and instructional practices that accommodate a range of student abilities, and explicit strategies to foster positive relationships among students. All of these elements are based on shared values that emphasize the importance of finding ways to enable students with varying abilities and interests to participate in shared learning experiences. Creating such a classroom requires making many modifications to the traditional ways that schools and classrooms have operated. In the following chapters, we examine strategies to make the necessary modifications without creating extraordinary or artificial barriers among students based on rigid perceptions of their abilities and disabilities.

Chapter 2

Accommodating Curricular and Instructional Practices in the Classroom

What teaching practices are most effective in inclusive classrooms, where students have a wide range of learning abilities and disabilities? Does the general education classroom teacher have to plan one lesson for the typical students and individual, adapted lessons for every student with an IEP? How can a teacher reach every student in the class without making the lesson boring for some students and too difficult for others? The basic methodology of effective teaching does not change in an inclusive classroom. A classroom that is effective for students with identified disabilities includes the same kind of curricular and instructional approaches that are effective for learners without identified disabilities (see Figure 2.1).

The accommodating curricular and instructional practices referred to in this chapter are those that have been demonstrated to be generally effective. Although it is a somewhat arbitrary distinction, we use the term *curriculum* to refer to *what* is taught—the learning goals or objectives for students. The term *instruction* is applied to the teaching *methods*—the grouping arrangements and instructional formats, the modes used to provide information or other input, and the ways that students practice their learning goals and demonstrate progress. It is important to make this distinction because when we discuss making individualized adaptations for particular students, we treat the curriculum content and the teaching methodology as two different aspects of the process.

The premise of our approach to teaching students with diverse learning needs is that rather than beginning our instructional planning by planning for most students—those without IEPs—and then adapting those plans for the students with identified learning differences, planning begins by considering what curricular and instructional approaches will encompass students' learning similarities. We begin with a universal approach to curriculum and instruction and then individualize as necessary. This concept is identical to the concept of universal design that guides the development of technology and architecture, which is having in increasingly greater impact on educational practice (see Figure 2.2). As illustrated in Figure 1.9, creating an inclusive school and classroom culture and utilizing accommodating curricular and instructional practices can effectively decrease the need for individualized adaptations.

What the Research Says

Research has provided empirical evidence to support the adage "good teaching is good teaching." Studies on instructional effectiveness in classrooms that included students with disabilities by Larivee (1985) and Mastropieri et al. (1998) found that classroom teachers who were generally effective for their students without disabilities also were effective teachers for their students with disabilities. The teachers whose students had higher academic achievement planned and delivered lessons that had the appropriate degree of difficulty and kept students actively engaged in learning. These teachers had well-organized classrooms where little time was lost in transitions, and they responded to students' mistakes and problem behaviors in ways that were supportive rather than punitive or critical.

When Vaughn, Gersten, and Chard (2000) synthesized the research on effective teaching methods for students with learning disabilities in inclusive classrooms, they also found that the methods that were effective in improving the achievement of students with learning disabilities were effective for their classmates without disabilities.

Research on effective teaching suggests that it makes sense to make improvements in teaching practices that will benefit all students, rather than limiting the focus to making adaptations or other interventions for specific students with disabilities.

Figure 2.1.   Good teaching is good teaching.

The Center for Applied Special Technology (CAST; 2003) has applied principles of universal design used in architecture and product design to create a new paradigm for teaching and learning that promotes these four assumptions:

- *Students with disabilities fall along a continuum of learner differences rather than consti-tuting a separate category.*
- *Teacher adjustments for learner differences should occur for all students, not just those with disabilities.*
- *Curriculum materials should be varied and diverse, including digital and on-line resources, rather than centering on a single textbook.*
- *Instead of remediating students so that they can learn from a set curriculum, curriculum should be made flexible to accommodate learner differences.*

The concept of universal design for learning suggests that, just as buildings and sidewalks need to be accessible for a wide variety of users, curricula and teaching methods should be flexible and adaptable for students with differing needs and abilities. For example, a standard social studies textbook limits the opportunities of a student who is dyslexic, who is blind, or for whom English is not the first language. However, the same material provided in a digital for-mat can be read aloud by a screen reader, printed in braille, translated into another lan-guage, or presented with highlighted main ideas. The digitally formatted social studies resource provides not only "access to information" but also "access to learning" (CAST, 2003).

Pisha and Coyne (2001) pointed out that curb cuts were originally designed to make buildings and sidewalks accessible for individuals who use wheelchairs. However, curb cuts are also useful to many people who do not have disabilities but are riding bikes, using strollers, or pushing carts. In the same way, universal design for learning incorporates flexibility in teach-ing methods that benefit many students, not only those with identified disabilities.

Figure 2.2.   The principle of universal design for learning.

In the following sections of this chapter, we describe six curricular and instructional approaches or methods that not only seem intuitively to be appropriate for inclusive classrooms but also have been demonstrated through research to have a positive impact on student achievement. Teachers with experi-ence in inclusive classrooms have found that planning for all students from the start—in addition to being a more genuine expression of the philosophy of inclusive education—also improves the efficiency of the planning process (see Figure 2.3).

MEANINGFUL, INTEGRATED CURRICULUM

When schoolwork is designed to help students to develop useful skills and knowledge and to achieve real purposes, interest and motiva-tion are increased. Attention is enhanced when the content is clearly connected with students' prior knowledge and experience and the ac-tivities are concrete and engaging (Mastro-pieri & Scruggs, 2004, p. 251). In addition to these benefits for attention and motivation, meaningful, integrated curriculum is consis-tent with the stated ultimate aim of schooling: to assist students to function effectively in their personal lives and as members of their communities. It makes sense not to leave the generalization and transfer of schooling to real life up to chance (see Figure 2.4).

Mastropieri and Scruggs (2004) reminded teachers that although all students are more motivated when the learning tasks in their classrooms are relevant and helpful to them, students with disabilities may be even more likely than their classmates to need direct ex-planations of why the tasks set before them are useful and important. They suggested the following ways to increase the likelihood that students will see learning as worthwhile and meaningful:

Voices from the Classroom

Cyndi Pitonyak, an elementary school special education consulting teacher, had worked for several years in a grade-level model for special education support. When they first started working within a grade-level model, Cyndi and the fifth-grade classroom teachers on her team felt that the grade-level model enhanced their collaboration by allowing them to meet together at weekly grade-level team meetings and reducing the number of special educators with whom the classroom teachers needed to consult. However, although Cyndi and her colleagues were able to do some collaborative planning at their weekly grade-level team meetings, Cyndi still had little time to meet with the individual fifth-grade teachers to actually plan collaboratively taught lessons or individualized adaptations for the students with IEPs. The team did not want to congregate the students with IEPs in certain classrooms in order to facilitate co-teaching and planning. They had been to many inservice workshops on making adaptations, co-teaching techniques, collaborative planning, and problem-solving skills, yet in reality, they were seldom able to schedule Cyndi into the classrooms.

The fifth-grade team and Cyndi realized, "Maybe we can go no further by simply manipulating the adults." Instead of trying to find the time for collaborative planning meetings (to plan co-taught lessons and individualized adaptations), the team decided to revise their approach to planning and to plan inclusively from the start. As Cyndi describes the process, "The fifth-grade team decided to engage in up-front, student-oriented planning. All planning includes all students. There is no 'regular' plan that is then adapted to meet individual needs. Activities are differentiated for all students from the beginning." The special education teacher became an integral part of planning with the grade-level teachers.

When the fifth-grade team evaluated their new special education model at the end of the school year, they unanimously agreed that, although work still needed to be done to improve the model, beginning from the premise that "all planning includes all students" was a sound approach to meeting all students' needs.

Figure 2.3.   When all planning includes all students.

- Select topics that reflect students' interests.
- Relate the content being studied to local issues or problems that are familiar and important to students.
- Allow students to select their assignment from a list of options.
- Begin and conclude classes with statements such as "This is an important topic because. . ." or questions such as "Why was this an important topic for us to learn about?" (Mastropieri & Scruggs, 2004, p. 251)

The fact that most teachers are now charged with teaching state and other learning standards that may not always bear obvious connections with students' life experiences does not mean that teachers must give up hope of creating relevant, meaningful curricula. Many states mandate only very broad outcomes for students in each of the major educational domains or disciplines. Even in states where the learning standards are expressed as more specific goals, these goals are intended to provide a framework for curriculum development, not to dictate what a teacher's weekly lesson plans must look like.

So, even if standard learning goals must be addressed, teachers can organize and teach the curriculum in ways that generate relevance for students. An *integrated or multidisciplinary curriculum approach*, with units organized around themes, issues, or problems rather than solely by disciplinary subject areas, is one tactic for maintaining authentic purposes and enhancing students' attention and engagement (Kovalik, 1997). Furthermore, if curriculum is structured around central unit themes or questions, students with differing abilities and learning styles can approach the unit using a variety of source materials, instructional methods, and modes of demonstrating their learning. Marzano suggested that one of the best ways for the teachers in a school to imple-

What the Research Says

Curriculum experts and school reformers agree that the answer to "What should the curriculum look like?" originates with the answer to "What kind of curriculum will best prepare students to function effectively as adults?" In other words, curriculum is based on what we want students to know and be able to do and on the kinds of values and outlooks we want students to have.

Resnick (1989) created the term *thinking curriculum* to refer to a curriculum that teaches students to use their content knowledge in real-world problem-solving and decision-making tasks. The thinking curriculum helps learners to do the type of thinking that is required by individuals performing tasks outside of school. Resnick observed that out-of-school thinking involves making decisions and solving problems about real-world events and situations. It typically involves groups of people who are involved in doing a task. The work is often aided by the use of tools, such as reference books and calculators and other technology. And it is typically interdisciplinary, involving many school subjects.

However, traditional curriculum models often emphasize isolated, low-level skills, especially for lower-achieving students. In contrast, the thinking curriculum includes content that goes beyond facts and definitions and includes concepts, principles, generalizations, and problems, as well as important processes such as learning strategies and skills, creative and critical thinking, metacognitive skills (i.e., skills used when thinking about thinking), and social skills (Resnick, 1989).

Educators Fennimore and Tinzmann (1990) at the North Central Regional Educational Laboratory (NCREL) suggested that, based on the qualities needed by adults in our society and on new research on learning, curriculum should be designed to create students who are:

- Knowledgeable: They have acquired a large and organized body of knowledge that they can use fluently to solve problems and make decisions,
- Self-determined: They view themselves as capable and eager learners,
- Strategic: They have an array of thinking and learning strategies that they use skillfully to control their own learning.
- Empathetic: They see themselves and the world from other perspectives, including those of people from different cultures.

The development of knowledgeable, self-determined, strategic, and empathic students is consistent with the theory and practice of inclusive education.

Figure 2.4. Developing a meaningful curriculum.

ment many of the elements of effective teaching is to organize curriculum content along with these research-based elements into a "framework for units" (2003, p. 85).

An integrated or multidisciplinary curriculum approach aids students in making the sorts of connections among subject areas that are required outside of school, promotes thinking and problem solving, and provides repeated practice in priority skills across the day. Integrated, thematic units are, of course, easier to utilize in elementary school, where individual teachers are responsible for teaching most of the major subject areas to their students. However, even in high school, where cross-disciplinary planning and teaching can be most difficult, problem-centered units that result in a culminating project that requires discipline-specific knowledge along with reading, writing, and higher-order thinking processes can be used to invigorate the curriculum and inspire students.

Unit themes should not just be clever or catchy but should focus on important issues and ideas that are central to the topic. Unit themes can be

- Political, environmental, social, historical, or personal problems
- Group or individual interests or hobbies
- Multifaceted projects relevant to the classroom, school, or community

Some examples of themes for integrated, multidisciplinary units and problem-centered, disciplinary units include the following:

- What Is Fair?
- Why Is the Population of Rockfish in the Chesapeake Bay Decreasing?
- Forms of Life in the Elementary School Courtyard Garden
- Webs Are for Spiders and for People

In Chapter 5, we provide an example of a unit planning format that can be used by teaching teams to plan instructional units (disciplinary or multidisciplinary) for mixed-ability classrooms. The process begins with identifying goals or outcomes for all students, including initial awareness of adapted goals for students who have IEPs. A kick-off activity establishes a shared motivating experience and focus among the students, and a culminating activity or project allows students to display their learning of the essential unit content in a variety of ways. Daily lessons using diverse methods, materials, instructional formats, and groupings are designed to keep all students involved in similar content and shared learning experiences but allow for individual differences.

When a class includes students with widely ranging abilities and disabilities, an integrated curriculum approach makes the differentiation of learning goals and tasks much simpler—and more inclusive—than planning separate lessons for some students. For example, one project in a fourth-grade interdisciplinary, thematic unit called "Forms of Life in the Elementary School Courtyard Garden" might be to inventory and classify the plants and animals living in the garden. This one project could involve learning goals in the areas of science (e.g., plant and animal identification and classification, animal habitat, plant growth requirements, use of a scientific method), math (e.g., measurement, graphing), reading and language arts (e.g., study of naturalist poetry and literature), and visual arts (e.g., drawings and paintings, study of

color and pattern). Students who have IEPs could either have simpler versions of the instructional objectives selected for most students (e.g., fewer vocabulary words, reading an easier book), or they could have objectives drawn from a different subject area (e.g., while most students are studying plant classification, a student with a severe disability might be organizing photographs of the courtyard garden's plants into categories by color, size, or shape). A curriculum that is rich in meaning and authentic in its purposes increases students' interest and motivation and lends itself to multiple types and levels of instructional goals.

APPROPRIATE INSTRUCTIONAL GOALS

Another hallmark of effective teaching is the thoughtful identification of instructional goals that are at a suitably high level of challenge for the student and are specific enough to be measured (Larivee, 1985; Mastropieri et al., 1998; Schmoker, 1999). The very first phase of designing curriculum that results in meaningful outcomes for students is the identification of goals. These goals should aim not only for the acquisition of isolated skills and knowledge but also for the achievement of principles, processes, and complex understanding of the topics covered (Wiggins & McTighe, 1998).

The research supporting the proposition that good teaching begins with identifying appropriate goals for students goes beyond the research on what effective individual teachers do and into the research on the qualities of effective schools. Effective schools have high expectations for *all* students (Reynolds & Teddlie, 2000), and they put those expectations into action by having clearly identified learning outcomes (Schmoker, 1999).

The best instructional goals are challenging but can be achieved with effort. Achievement is actually enhanced when students experience *optimal challenge,* that is, goals that are high but also realistic (Ford, 1995). Involving students in setting goals and monitoring their success also can increase achievement (Locke & Latham, 1990).

In inclusive classrooms, all students have clearly identified learning goals, but not all students have the same goals. The universal design for learning that is advocated in this chapter calls for considering the individualized goals of students with IEPs from the outset. This means that initial instructional planning requires general and special education teachers to be aware of both the required general education learning standards and the IEP goals of individual students.

ACTIVE LEARNING

Lessons that incorporate such activities as demonstrations, simulations, experiments, applied learning stations, role-playing, and community-based projects help to ensure that students have opportunities to become actively engaged in the learning process. Activity-based lessons are designed to provide instruction within the context of an authentic, hands-on activity. Activity-oriented (in contrast with textbook-oriented) approaches to science and social studies have been shown to promote learning for students with disabilities when appropriate modifications and support are provided (Scruggs & Mastropieri, 1993).

Kovalik (1997) advocated keeping instruction as close as possible to real world experiences. As indicated in Figure 2.5, Kovalik's theory suggests that a lesson involving the manipulation of concrete objects has greater instructional power than one that only involves manipulating representational objects or symbols, but real world experiences are the most powerful of all. As Confuscius said,

What I hear, I forget.

What I see, I remember.

What I do, I understand.

An activity-oriented, hands-on approach stands in contrast to teaching that uses only lectures, worksheets, and other more passive instructional formats. For example, the concept of equivalent liquid measures using cups, quarts, and gallons can be explained through a lecture and demonstration, following which students complete a worksheet that requires them to complete statements such as "One quart equals _____ cups" or to match pictures of various measuring containers holding equivalent amounts. However, students' attention and understanding would be enhanced by following the lecture and demonstration with an activity involving the use of liquid measuring devices to solve a series of equivalency problems, to make fruit juice from concentrate to serve to the class, or to fill the classroom aquarium. Students might later complete the worksheet on equivalent measures but not before they had experience with a concrete activity.

---

1. *Being there:* The student is there, through field trips or community-based instruction.
2. *Immersion:* The learning environment all around the student in many forms.
3. *Hands on the real thing:* Real objects to observe and manipulate are right in front of the student.
4. *Hands on representational objects:* The student has imitation objects to observe and manipulate.
5. *Second hand:* Somebody else has had an experience and tells the student about it or shows it to the student.
6. *Symbolic:* The student is exposed to and manipulates words and numbers.

Figure 2.5. Choices of instructional input for maximum motivation and achievement. (*Source:* Kovalik, 1997)

It is important to remember, however, that these hands-on activities must be structured to keep students focused on the purpose and procedures of the activity. As Wiggins and McTighe (1998) noted, meaningful learning requires "minds-on" and not only "hands-on" activities. Completing the activity is not the goal of the lesson; the activity is used as a vehicle for engaging students in learning the essential content and concepts that have been targeted. For example, consider again the hands-on activity of filling the classroom aquarium. Instructional input on measurement (definitions, examples, and demonstrations) should be provided for the students before they undertake the actual task of filling the aquarium; feedback should be provided following the activity; and additional independent practice should be provided at a later time. Simply getting the aquarium filled is not the primary purpose of the lesson. Learning about measurement is.

Activity-based lessons are advantageous in inclusive classrooms for a number of reasons. First, hands-on, active learning is more beneficial than passive learning for many students. It not only gives practical meaning to otherwise abstract content but also assists students to construct knowledge through manipulation of interactive materials and primary data sources. Students with less sophisticated cognitive abilities and students who need visual, tactile, or kinesthetic input especially benefit from interacting with concrete activities. Besides enhancing student interest and motivation, activity-based lessons make it easier to address a range of learning goals within shared activities. In a group of students with the task of filling the classroom aquarium, two students might calculate how many quarts or cups of water it will take to fill the 10-gallon tank, two students might calculate the metric equivalence of those amounts, and another student might count the number of quarts of water poured into the tank. Remember, too, that if this activity is part of an integrated, thematic unit, science content and language arts skills on a variety of levels can be embedded in the activity as well.

None of this is to say that skill-based instruction is not also important and necessary in an inclusive class- *room.* Students with and without IEPs also need direct instruction in specific skills and knowledge, along with adequate drill and practice in using those skills and knowledge. However, the end goal of learning is for students to be able to apply their skills and knowledge in a variety of meaningful contexts. Providing instructional activities that allow students to apply skills from several domains in practical contexts can enhance motivation, attention, retention, and generalization.

MULTIPLE MODALITIES

Listening and reading are often the primary modalities for sharing information in classrooms. Student achievement is enhanced when teachers use multiple modalities to present content (Marzano, 1998). These modalities range from the use of graphic organizers (e.g., concept maps, webs, Venn diagrams) and other visual strategies (e.g., timelines, drawings, pictographs, graphs, physical models) to music and kinesthetic activities. (Marzano referred to these instructional strategies as "nonlinguistic representations.") In addition to helping teachers to stay focused on their essential instructional goals and the relationships among them, visual strategies can help students to "make their thinking visible" (Burke, 1994, p. 118).

McTighe and Lyman listed the following six purposes for using graphic organizers:

1. Represent abstract information in a more concrete form
2. Represent relationships between and among facts and concepts
3. Generate and organize ideas for writing
4. Relate new information to prior knowledge
5. Store and retrieve information
6. Assess student thinking and learning (1992, p. 81)

Graphic organizers (see Figure 2.6) are effective instructional tools even when merely used by the teacher as a way to anchor students' attention and provide an aide for understanding concepts and processes or remembering information and how it is organized.

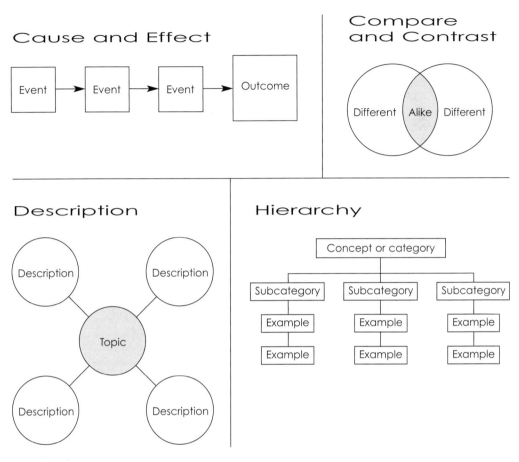

Figure 2.6. Graphic organizers.

However, graphic organizers can have an even more powerful effect when students are actually taught the structure and purpose of the strategy so that they can apply it themselves to current and future learning tasks. When first using a graphic organizer, such as a concept map, teachers can model its use for students and then have students practice using the strategy with familiar topics. Appendix B lists some helpful resources on the use of graphic organizers and other visual strategies.

COOPERATIVE LEARNING

Because of the positive effects on motivation, academic achievement, and social acceptance, *cooperative learning* is among the instructional strategies most frequently recommended for use by teachers in inclusive classrooms (Johnson & Johnson, 1999; Nevin, Thousand, & Villa, 1994; Putnam, 1993; Sapon-Shevin, Ayres, & Duncan, 1994). Often used in combination with activity-based learning and other support strategies, cooperative learning has been reported to reduce the need for multiple adaptations (see Figure 2.7).

Both the philosophy and the structure of cooperative learning are well suited to inclusive classrooms. Cooperative learning teaches students to work together toward common goals and to value the range of contributions that can be made by individual group members. Johnson and Johnson (1999), two of the foremost experts in the development of cooperative learning, described these five essential components of cooperative learning:

What the Research Says

Cooperative learning groups organizes students into teams so that they work together as a group toward common learning goals. A significant amount of research offers reasons for using cooperative learning groups and ideas and tips for how to do it well.

Why Use Cooperative Learning Groups?

- Increased academic engagement and achievement
- Increased social skills
- Less disruption and more focus on task behavior
- Allowance for differentiation of tasks
- Ability to ensure that all students have a chance to make a contribution

How Should Students Be Grouped for Cooperative Learning?

- Small groups: three or four students per group is optimal
- Mostly homogeneous groups (flexible ability groups based on acquisition of a particular prerequisite skill may be used in moderation)
- Three types of groups: informal, formal, and base groups (i.e., ongoing groups that serve as a homebase for a semester or year)
- A variety of criteria for forming heterogeneous groups: modality preferences, alphabetical order, shared interests or hobbies, common experiences

Figure 2.7.   Why and how to use cooperative learning groups. (*Sources:* Johnson, Maruyama, Johnson, Nelson, & Skon, 1981; Lew, Mesch, Johnson, & Johnson, 1986; Lou, Abrami, Spence, Paulsen, Chambers, & d'Apollonio, 1996; Slavin, 1992)

1. *Positive interdependence:* Group tasks are structured so that students need to rely on one another for the group to reach its goals. For example, each student fills a role in the group (e.g., facilitator, recorder, reporter, materials manager, "scout") and completes a particular part of the task. Teachers also can structure the task itself in ways that promote positive interdependence, such as by providing each group with only one set of materials.

2. *Individual accountability:* Although the group as a whole is responsible for achieving its goal, each member is also responsible for doing his or her part and for helping all group members to meet their learning objectives.

3. *Heterogeneous grouping:* Groupings typically maximize differences in ability and personal characteristics rather than minimize the range of skill or ability levels within

the group. In many classrooms where cooperative learning is practiced, not only do students belong to base groups with whom they work repeatedly, but they also may be grouped in a variety of other ways—by interest, gender, or prerequisite skills—depending on the nature of the specific activity.

4. *Direct instruction of social skills:* The teacher actively teaches the social interaction and task-related skills required for the group to function effectively. Students are instructed in the use of effective communication and collaboration skills such as listening, encouraging one another, and negotiating conflicts. Teachers observe, evaluate, and provide feedback on the use of group skills.

5. *Group processing:* In addition to assessing how well they completed the task, groups are provided with structures to help them

assess and improve their ability to communicate and work together. For example, at the end of the activity, each group might complete a self-evaluation instrument that includes questions about how well group members filled their roles and whether specified collaborative skills were performed.

Effective inclusive classrooms use both formal cooperative learning and informal peer cooperation as integral aspects of the classroom structure and culture. Cooperative learning will have little impact on students if it is practiced only during a few designated activities or if tasks are not structured to facilitate positive interdependence and students do not receive adequate instruction in the necessary skills to work cooperatively. In applying the method to inclusive classrooms, keep in mind that basing all small groups on a fixed decision about students' abilities will not achieve the goal of social and instructional interaction among students with and without disabilities. Instead, base student groupings on a variety of dimensions, depending on the purpose and nature of the task.

The use of cooperative learning and peer tutoring as instructional methods for inclusive classrooms is covered more fully in *Social Relationships and Peer Supports* (Snell & Janney, 2000), another volume in the *Teachers' Guides to Inclusive Practices* series. A number of valuable references on cooperative learning are provided in the resource list in Appendix B.

SYSTEMATIC LESSON STRUCTURE

An effective lesson is one that is at an appropriate level of difficulty, keeps students actively engaged in the task, includes supportive teacher–student interactions, and makes efficient use of time (Larivee, 1985). Although a number of models for designing effective, well-structured lessons are available, most include elements similar to the following (Hunter, 1984):

- *Anticipatory set* (sometimes called *structuring*). In this phase, the teacher creates readiness and interest in the lesson by connecting the lesson to previous learning and relating the purpose or objective of the current lesson.

- *Presentation/instructional input.* This is the heart of the lesson, in which new information is provided clearly using a variety of modalities, and new skills or processes are demonstrated or modeled. Before moving on to practice activities, the teacher completes a check for understanding to ensure that students have comprehended the material.

- *Sufficient practice.* The first stage is guided practice, when new content, skills, or processes are practiced with the teacher's immediate guidance and feedback; then comes independent practice, when students practice on their own, with delayed feedback.

- *Closure and evaluation.* Before moving on to the next lesson, the teacher reviews what was learned and engages the students in evaluating their learning.

- *Application with generalization or transfer.* In later lessons, the teacher provides opportunities to apply the content, skills, or process in new and increasingly complex contexts.

Of course, merely using these elements to structure a lesson does not ensure effective teaching. Within this structure, effective teachers in inclusive classrooms 1) give clear presentations, 2) use redundancy to reinforce key concepts, 3) are enthusiastic, and 4) progress at an appropriate rate by teaching in small steps and giving students a lot of successful practice and helpful feedback after each step. They keep students engaged by selecting motivating, multimodal materials and posing questions in ways that require active responding from most students (Mastropieri & Scruggs, 2002).

Voices from the Classroom

Lynn Graves is a second-grade classroom teacher in a fully inclusive school. She team-teaches with another second-grade teacher and a special education teacher (who also serves students in two other second-grade classrooms). Since she has been teaching in an inclusive school, Ms. Graves has learned to use teaching approaches and organizational strategies that accommodate her diverse group of students. Some of these practices were initiated for her students with disabilities but have become part of Ms. Graves's regular teaching practices. Ms. Graves sums up her teaching approach in this way: "My goal is for people to walk in and not be able to recognize who has a disability. Everyone has a way to contribute in our class." A few of Ms. Graves's inclusive teaching strategies are listed below.

Teaching Methods

- Thematic, multidisciplinary units that encompass the basic skills and content areas
- Hands-on lessons, using the multiple intelligences
- Learning stations for each unit, with some stations directed by parent volunteers
- Allowing and encouraging many different ways for students to respond and demonstrate learning (e.g., written reports, slide shows, posters)
- Lots of small groups, including both ability grouping and mixed ability grouping. For reading, students are grouped by reading level into novel groups. The two second-grade teachers and the special education teacher rotate groups at the end of each novel. The three teachers do station teaching for math, technology, science, and social studies. Students are assigned to heterogeneous groups or are sometimes grouped by interests.
- Pairing students with fifth-grade peer tutors for tutoring sessions twice per week.

Organizational Tools for Students

- A desk folder for each student in which work-in-progress is kept until it is turned in to the "Finished Work Basket"
- Steps of the writing process listed on a large poster and also in each student's writing notebook and the teacher's model writing notebook
- Students shown how to use prewriting strategies such as webbing
- A laminated checklist for each student with the daily schedule written on it. Students check off each activity as it is completed. Some students have an additional task card with the subtasks that they are to complete for each activity
- Grading rubrics supplied for projects, major assignments, and tests
- Student-drawn maps of the inside of their desks that help them keep materials organized

Classroom Management

- Community-building activities on ways that students are alike and ways that they are different; group problem-solving sessions about social and behavioral difficulties
- Classroom behavioral expectations taught through explanation, demonstration, prompting, and reinforcement. The classroom rules are listed on a large poster under the title "The Way We Want Our Class to Be." In periodic class meetings, students discuss their "Successes" and "Rough Spots," which Ms. Graves lists at the bottom of the poster
- Lots of movement, including using music, clapping, singing, and miming during transitions from one activity to the next

Figure 2.8.   A teacher tells how inclusion has affected her teaching.

SUMMARY

All of these methods and strategies taken together—meaningful integrated curriculum, appropriate instructional goals, multiple modalities, active learning, cooperative learning, and systematic lesson structure—make it easier for teachers to create learning activities in which students with varying abilities can participate together. Instructional activities that are motivating, engaging, and meaningful tend to be those that are accessible at varying levels of difficulty. Although individualized adaptations still will be required for some students, if instructional unit and lesson planning begins with the use of accommodating curricular and instructional practices, the need for later adaptations is decreased.

In addition, if the culture and climate of the classroom are such that individual differences are accepted and valued, then difference becomes ordinary and the stigma of individualized supports and adaptations is decreased. Classroom teachers have reported that teaching in an inclusive setting broadens their repertoire of teaching approaches and methods, making them better teachers for all of their students (see Figure 2.8).

Chapter 3

A Model for Making Adaptations

This chapter describes a model for making individualized adaptations to schoolwork in inclusive classrooms. The model includes a distinction among three types of adaptations: 1) curricular adaptations (content and goals), 2) instructional adaptations (methods, materials, technology and other supports), and 3) alternative adaptations (an individualized activity focused on specific IEP goals). The model also entails making adaptations in two stages: 1) general adaptations that stay in place for a period of time and 2) specific adaptations that vary from day to day. The model is based on the belief that adaptations should meet two criteria. They should achieve both social and instructional participation and be only as special as necessary.

WHAT IS A MODEL AND WHY IS IT NECESSARY?

A model for making adaptations is a framework for thinking about the entire process of designing, using, and evaluating individualized adaptations. A model can be useful because it enables teachers to view this sometimes complex process in a way that allows them to apply it to a variety of individual students. To illustrate the need for a model, think of a typical instructional activity in most elementary school classrooms, such as oral reading groups. It would not take long to brainstorm dozens of ways to modify reading groups: read an easier book, provide a large-print book, decrease the number of students in the group, assign shorter passages to read, schedule a shorter period of time for reading and increase the amount of time spent in preparation for reading, and so forth. However, the challenge of adapting schoolwork is not simply in generating ideas but in the selection of adaptations that are appropriate for individual students and feasible within a given classroom situation. In order to develop appropriate individualized adaptations for their students, teachers need a process to apply in any situation, not simply a list of possible adaptations from which to choose.

One reason that merely providing a list or array of possible adaptations does not work is that no list could possibly address the needs of every student. A model, however, can provide a process, including a series of guidelines and decision-making rules, that can be used to address the needs of any student who has been identified as having special learning needs. In addition, using a model is consistent with the IEP process, whereby a student's individual learning goals, accommodations, services, and supports are considered.

A second reason for having a model for making adaptations relates to the need for collaboration in inclusive classrooms. No longer is one teacher responsible for planning, teaching, and evaluating instruction for an entire class. Now, one or more teachers, along with one or more additional staff members, may share these responsibilities. Teamwork can be hindered when team members have not clarified the steps involved in doing their work, such as determining how decisions will be made and who will do which action steps. Having a model helps teams to discuss their work using a common language and to reach a shared understanding of what tasks are required of them.

PREREQUISITES FOR THE MODEL

As described in Chapter 1, this model for making adaptations assumes that the students for whom adaptations are being made are attending inclusive schools. That is, they are enrolled in neighborhood schools, are based in general education homerooms and classes, and are being educated by collaborating teams of general and special education teachers. Also, it assumes that effective, evidence-based curricular and instructional practices, such as those described in Chapter 2, are being put into place as part of the ongoing effort to create a truly inclusive classroom.

Two additional prerequisites for this model pertain to the IEPs of the students for whom individualized adaptations are being made. First, the model assumes that students' IEP

One of the most significant changes to the 1997 reauthorization of the Individuals with Disabilities Education Act (IDEA) of 1990 was an increased emphasis upon the participation of students with disabilities in the general curriculum and the general education classroom and the provision of the supplementary aids and services necessary for appropriate participation in various areas of the curriculum.

For example, according to the IDEA Amendments of 1997 (PL 105-17), the "present levels of educational performance" section of the IEP must now include a statement of how the child's disability affects his or her involvement and progress in the general curriculum. Also, the "free, appropriate public education" section of the IEP must contain a statement of special education and related services, as well as the supplementary aids and services, that the child or youth needs in order to

Be involved and progress in the general curriculum . . . and to participate in extracurricular and other nonacademic activities; and . . . to be educated and participate with other children with disabilities and nondisabled children. . . . (Section 614[d][1] [A][iii])

Another change in the law is that each student's IEP must now include a statement of how the administration of state- or districtwide assessments will be modified for the student. If the IEP team determines that the student cannot participate in such assessments, then the IEP must include a statement of 1) why the assessment is not appropriate for the child and 2) how the child will be assessed.

Figure 3.1. The Individuals with Disabilities Education Act (IDEA) Amendments of 1997 (PL 105-17) and the general education curriculum. (From National Information Center for Children and Youth with Disabilities. [1998]. *The IDEA Amendments of 1997* [News Digest 26]. Washington, DC: Author.)

goals are drawn directly from or are linked to the general curriculum. Regardless of how divergent a student's learning goals are from those of his or her classmates, the IEP process has identified IEP goals that dovetail with state or school district learning standards (see Figure 3.1).

The second IEP-related prerequisite for this adaptations model is that students' IEPs must include accommodations to teaching and testing that enable these students to make and demonstrate progress toward their learning goals—whether those goals come directly from the general curriculum standards or are individualized. Another way to express this requirement is to say that students' IEPs must provide access to a free, appropriate public education (FAPE) in the least restrictive environment (LRE), as specified in the IDEA and its amendments.

To clarify this statement, consider the difference between accommodations and adaptations. The term *accommodations* is used to refer to changes to the school program that are documented by the eligibility process and specified in a student's IEP. Accommodations are provided to enable the student to gain access to the classroom or the curriculum. Accommodations might include giving the student extra time to complete a test, allowing the student to sit close to the chalkboard, not counting spelling errors during in-class tests, or providing the student with the assistive technology necessary to compensate for a sensory or motor disability.

In contrast, *adaptations* are changes that are made to learning task requirements, teaching methods and materials, or the physical environment when the IEP is already in place. Often, these changes are temporary or reduced over time. Examples of adaptations include providing a student with objects to count in order to complete a math problem that classmates are doing with paper and pencil or requiring a student to demonstrate a targeted social skill rather than write an essay describing what he or she would do in a hypothetical situation.

It is important for all team members who work with a student to be aware of the IEP accommodations for which a student qualifies and to understand that decisions about learning goals and accommodations are made by the IEP team and documented on the IEP. Once an accommodation is specified in a student's IEP, it is part of the student's FAPE. Information about the student's IEP goals and accommodations is available prior to many of the decisions that need to be made on a semester-long, weekly, or daily basis about how specific lessons and activities will be adapted. In contrast, decisions about IEP accommodations typically are not made as a function of a teacher's planning for a particular class period or lesson. They are made as a function of the multidisciplinary IEP process and should be based on data regarding the student's disability that were gleaned through the diagnostic assessment process.

In other words, in this adaptations model, IEP goals and accommodations are taken as givens that must be considered when deciding whether and how to make further adaptations. These adaptations, including the specific ways that an adapted curriculum will be coordinated or integrated with the general class curriculum, are determined through ongoing team planning based on the parameters provided by the IEP.

Therefore, for example, if a student is capable of participating fully in the general curriculum given that accommodations such as more time to complete written assignments, a separate room for taking tests, or having directions read aloud are provided, then the student may not require many individualized adaptations. However, the student does need to receive those IEP accommodations whenever necessary. The student may also need skill development or remediation to reduce the need for those accommodations in the future.

CRITERIA FOR MAKING INDIVIDUALIZED ADAPTATIONS

The most effective adaptations facilitate both social and instructional participation in class activities. That is, learning activities can and should be designed so that students with varying abil-

ities work together within shared activities. One goal of inclusive education is for students with IEPs to be full members of their schools and classroom groups and to participate in the ongoing social life of the classroom. Another goal is for students to achieve academic and functional competence at a variety of activities that are suitable for them. Although all students should be included with their age peers for social purposes, just being present, or being included for what is often referred to as *socialization,* is not enough. Students must make progress toward specific learning goals, whether those goals involve social, academic, motor, or personal aspects of education.

Therefore, adaptations ideally are designed not only to keep the student busy or present with classmates but also to enable the student to practice and master relevant instructional goals. Students' goals will range from being slightly different to vastly different from their classmates' curriculum goals. The adaptations designed for students with very different curriculum goals should enable them to take an active part in instructional activities, even if their participation is designed to achieve a different learning goal from that of classmates.

Student Snapshot

 Melanie, a fourth grader, has autism. She reads some; writes some words and phrases using a computer; and communicates through a combination of words, gestures, and symbols. Melanie writes very little and very reluctantly. During a science lesson, she is given the same water cycle worksheet as her classmates. Other students are using a word bank to label the stages in the water cycle that are depicted on the worksheet. Should Melanie be given a crayon to use to color the water cycle? (She may simply scribble all over the sheet.) Or should the words from the word bank be written on adhesive labels that she can peel off and use to identify the stages of the water cycle?

Student Snapshot

Daniel, a first-grade student, has multiple disabilities, including cerebral palsy and mental retardation. During calendar time, Daniel is positioned on a wedge on the floor with his classmates. His goal is to attend to the speaker as his teacher poses a series of questions to classmates. Could a simple, two-switch speech device be programmed so that Daniel could answer a predictable question posed by the teacher?

Student Snapshot

Walter's eleventh-grade English class is working in cooperative groups to complete a term project on a famous author. Walter's assigned role is to be the checker, checking off the group's tasks on the assignment sheet as each step is com-pleted. Instead, could Walter also be gathering information for the group but be provided with a list of reference sources at his readability level?

Teachers may sometimes find themselves questioning the value of adapting an activity that seems to be distant from the functional skill needs of a student with a severe disability. But remember that functionality is only one criterion for selecting IEP goals and objectives. Other valid criteria for selecting learning outcomes include student or family preference, use of age-appropriate activities, and the opportunity to increase the student's social participation and interaction. The two priorities—social and instructional participation—need to be balanced (see Figure 3.2). At times, teachers may have to make a choice to emphasize one or the other for a particular activity, but they also can continue to try to determine how to move closer to accomplishing both.

What the Research Says

Several research studies have shown that students with disabilities must participate in ongoing classroom routines and activities in order to be viewed as full members of their classroom group. Schnorr (1990) found that first-graders defined their school experience on the basis of themes that centered on sharing the same class assignments, activities, and peer networks. Peter, a student with mental retardation who was mainstreamed part time, was not perceived by his peers to be a class member because "he did not share in the first-grade experience as defined by these students" (Schnorr, 1990, p. 38). Instead, Peter was perceived as a visitor and had little chance of developing a friendship with the other students because friends, as defined by these students, were members of the same class. Similarly, Peck, Gallucci, Staub, and Schwartz found that "The children we interviewed consistently expressed the view that mere physical presence did not mean a child was a real member of the class. What was critical was participation" (1998, p. 8).

Janney and Snell (1997) also found support for the theory that it is participation in shared lessons—even with the use of adaptations—that defines *inclusion*. In a study of the peer supports used in several inclusive elementary classes, the authors found that peers could describe the sorts of adaptations provided for their classmates with moderate and severe disabilities but still viewed these classmates as doing "the same work." For example, when asked, "Does Peter [a student with mental retardation] do the same work?" a classmate replied, "He does the same thing, but he doesn't write that much." In fact, Peter did very little reading or writing, but he did participate in functional academic tasks within activities that were quite similar to those of his classmates.

And, in their synthesis of 20 studies that examined the perceptions of elementary and secondary students with high-incidence disabilities and their typical peers on the instruction occurring in inclusive classrooms, Klingner and Vaughn (1999) confirmed that both groups of students wanted to have the same activities, books, homework, grading criteria, and grouping practices.

Figure 3.2. Belonging requires participation.

The most effective adaptations are only as special as necessary. The adaptations teachers or IEP teams create should not be more intrusive than necessary in order to enable the student to participate in classroom activities. The goal is not to conceal individual differences or to pretend that they do not exist. In fact, students without disabilities should have opportunities to learn to appreciate individual differences and to understand that equality does not require that everyone be treated identically. However, no one wants to be singled out to receive special treatment all of the time, and receiving extra assistance or adapted instruction should not require removing a student from opportunities to engage in typical activities and to develop such ordinary relationships as friendships and acquaintances with a variety of people. Such treatment can interfere with the development of peer acceptance, self-confidence, and independence (see Table 3.1).

An "only as special as necessary" approach to adaptations suggests altering only the elements of the lesson or activity necessary to enable the student to participate actively in meeting IEP objectives and altering those elements in the least extraordinary way possible. As Strickland and Turnbull (1990) noted, the specialness or intrusiveness of an adaptation is determined from the student's perspective. The ideal is to create adaptations that deviate as little as possible from the ordinary, yet enable the student to benefit from the activity. This type of adaptation is not always easiest from the teacher's perspective, as it often requires a change in teacher behavior rather than in what the student does or in the materials provided for the student.

The "only as special as necessary" guideline also reminds teachers and IEP teams that they should not assume that the student needs a teacher or instructional assistant by her or his side at every minute or that the goals or materials for each and every lesson must always be adapted. Furthermore, adapting an activity does not require sitting at a table at the back of the room: Adaptations can be provided alongside classmates, within the context of ongoing classroom activities.

Another way to keep adaptations as unintrusive as possible is to think of them as supports that are provided for students to help them to be successful. The support will often be temporary or faded out over time as the student acquires new competencies to cope with challenges. Receiving too much support interferes with the development of self-control and self-determination, as does receiving too little support.

THE MODEL: THREE TYPES OF ADAPTATIONS

Every lesson or instructional activity has several elements that can be adapted so that a student can participate in a way that is personally meaningful. Our model organizes these elements into three major categories of adaptations: curricular, instructional, and alternative (see Table 3.2). Knowing the types of adaptations that a student needs can help the team to know when and how to plan the student's adaptations and to keep the adaptations from becoming too intrusive.

Curricular Adaptations: Individualizing the Learning Goal

In an inclusive classroom, the scope and sequence of the curriculum are broadened to accommodate a greater range of student learning goals. The traditional general education

Table 3.1. "Only as special as necessary" approach to adaptations

Student's need for specialization	Student's common ground with others
Adaptive equipment	Regular lives
Related therapy services	Ordinary relationships
Adapted curriculum	Everyday activities
Specialize instruction	Typical places
Modified materials	Common events

Table 3.2. Types of adaptations

Type	How it's done
Curricular	Alter the content of what is taught
Instructional	Alter how content is taught and/or how learning is demonstrated
Alternative	Alter the goal, the instruction, and the activity

Table 3.3. Types of curricular adaptations

Type	How it's done
Supplementary	Add social-behavioral, communication, study, and/or self-management skills to the general curriculum
Simplified	Change the level of difficulty or include fewer goals
Alternative	Teach functional skills plus embedded social, communication, and motor skills through participation in age-appropriate activities

curriculum includes the following subjects or goal areas:

- Basic skills (reading, writing, math)
- Content areas (social studies, science)
- The arts
- Physical and health education

To accommodate all learners with exceptional needs, the curriculum in an inclusive classroom must be expanded in scope so that it also includes the following:

- Functional skills for use in daily life at home, at school, at work, and in the community

- Functional academic skills (e.g., using money, counting, telling time) needed to perform daily routines

- Social-behavioral, communication, motor, study/organizational, and self-management skills that are used across the day in a variety of different activities, subjects, and places (These related or embedded skills are also referred to as cross-environmental skills [e.g., Giangreco, Cloninger, & Iverson, 1998].)

It would be ideal to imagine a school in which all students participate in whatever areas and levels of inclusive curriculum are appropriate for them. However, in actuality, curriculum adaptation is usually conceived as a change to the traditional general education curriculum. The typical general education curriculum can be adapted in three ways to meet the individual needs of students—

by supplementing, simplifying, or altering the curriculum (see Table 3.3).

Supplementary Curriculum Goals

Some students with IEPs participate fully in the general education curriculum but require supplementary IEP goals in one or more subject or goal areas. Typical areas for supplementary curriculum goals include basic skills (e.g., reading, writing, math) or skills that are applied across the day (e.g., social skills, study skills, learning strategies). Students whose curricular goals are adapted primarily by supplementing the general education curriculum would most often be those students identified as having a learning disability or an emotional or behavioral disorder rather than those who have an intellectual disability or severe multiple disabilities.

Student Snapshot

Vanessa is a 13-year-old who attends seventh grade at her local middle school. She has a learning disability in reading and written language but is enrolled in a typical schedule of seventh-grade courses. She has a study hall/tutorial session each day, as do her classmates. She uses the time this session provides to complete tests and assignments and to receive instruction and as-

sistance in doing written assignments. Vanessa participates fully in the general academic curriculum with supplementary curriculum adaptations in writing processes and study skills. Virtually all of the modifications made to her instruction are actually accommodations that provide her with extra time, copies of teachers' notes or note-taking assistance, a laptop computer for taking notes, books on tape, oral testing for essay questions, and no penalties for spelling and grammar errors on in-class work. Beyond these special services and her IEP accommodations, Vanessa requires virtually no ongoing adaptations.

Simplified Curriculum Goals

Other students with IEPs participate in the traditional subject areas, but their instructional goals are simplified. That is, their goals are drawn from a lower grade level or require less complex types of learning (e.g., a student might memorize facts or apply a concept, whereas classmates without disabilities might have goals requiring analysis or evaluation of the material). Curriculum goals can also be simplified by emphasizing fewer skills and concepts rather than the entire scope of the general curriculum.

Student Snapshot

 Sam is 14 years old and attends ninth grade at his local high school. He is a highly articulate young man who has characteristics of pervasive developmental disorder and obsessive-compulsive disorder. Sam has a wide range of academic skills; his vocabulary skills, reading comprehension, and general knowledge are his strengths, whereas he finds math and other skill areas that require close attention and decision making to be more challenging. Sam's schedule includes general-level academic courses and electives that allow Sam to explore vocational options. Sam receives full-time special education instruction and support, including six periods per day of pull-in support from a special education teacher or assistant and one period per day of direct instruction in a resource setting. Curriculum adaptations for Sam involve

simplifying the content by eliminating technical, conceptually difficult, or confusing material. Because of his curricular modifications, Sam will be a candidate for an IEP diploma rather than an academic diploma.

Alternative Curriculum Goals

A third approach to curricular adaptation involves changing to alternative, functional curriculum goals (Ford et al., 1989; Peterson, LeRoy, Field, & Wood, 1992). Such curricular goals emphasize the skills needed to participate in high-priority activities in the five community-living domains or goal areas: 1) general community use, 2) domestic (or home living) and self-management (or self-help), 3) recreational, 4) vocational skills, and 5) school. We also include school as one of the community-living domains because a community-referenced curriculum is determined by assessing the environments in which a student participates. School-age students spend a significant portion of their day at school, and many students who have cognitive or physical disabilities actually need instruction in order to participate in the functional skills and routines that are required throughout the day (e.g., arrival and departure routines, using the school media center, eating in the cafeteria). A functional, community-referenced curriculum also includes the functional academic skills (e.g., reading, writing, money and time management) needed to participate in activities in the community-living domains. For some students, emphasis is placed on the motor, social, and communication skills that will increase their participation in targeted school and community activities (see Rainforth, York, & Macdonald, 1992).

Students whose IEPs include altered curriculum goals are most often those who are classified as having mental retardation requiring limited to extensive supports in cognitive tasks (or what is often described as mental retardation in the moderate to severe range) and those who have severe, multiple disabilities. Although these students have a wide range of individual learning needs, they share the learning characteristics of acquiring new skills and information more slowly and therefore learning less than their typical peers. They also have difficulty in generalizing and transferring what they have learned under one set of conditions to new settings and conditions. What these learning characteristics imply is that students with cognitive disabilities should be taught important, useful, meaningful skills and knowledge, and they should be taught and tested under the conditions where they will ultimately need to use those skills and knowledge. In other words, they need meaningful curriculum goals that will help them to function in the community as adults, and they need hands-on learning experiences with concrete materials and learning trials that do not waste time by allowing the student to practice making errors.

Even students with the most severe disabilities can participate to some degree in most of the ongoing routines and activities in a typical classroom. Indeed, one of the most common adaptations made for students who have severe or multiple disabilities is to apply the *principle of partial participation* (Baumgart et al., 1982). This principle suggests that individuals who have disabilities should not be deprived of opportunities to participate in typical school and community activities simply because they cannot participate fully or independently in those activities. The fact that a student may not be able to do every part of an activity does not mean that some level of participation in that activity would not be valuable to the student.

Student Snapshot

Daniel can speak a few words. He has some purposeful movement of his arms and hands but needs physical assistance to perform most daily living and self-help activities. He can take a few steps with assistance, but a wheelchair is his primary means of transportation. Daniel's alternative curriculum adaptations emphasize embedded motor and communication skills, partial participation in self-help routines and group

activities, and some simplified reading and arithmetic objectives. Rather than providing a separate functional or community-based instruction program, Daniel's instruction in functional skills and routines is integrated into the general education program. Because of Daniel's physical needs, an assistant is assigned to the classroom throughout the day. The assistant positions Daniel in a variety of ways to keep him comfortable and close to his peers and provides the physical assistance that he needs to find objects and to orient himself.

One caution regarding a functional curriculum is that many things that students can and should learn are not functional in the strictest sense of the word. For example, many students who have some alternative, functional curricular goals can benefit from learning general facts and knowledge, which, although not necessarily essential for being able to participate in functional daily routines, are nonetheless nice to know. Melanie, for example, has many functional goals on her IEP, but her parents and teachers also believed it was important for Melanie to have the following goal on her IEP: "For each unit taught in social studies, Melanie will write, read, spell, and use in class activities four or five key concepts or vocabulary words." These key terms were to be selected by Melanie's special education and general education teachers as part of the collaborative planning done by the fourth-grade team for each social studies unit.

Choosing Appropriate Curricular Adaptations

If a student's learning goals vary from those specified in the general curriculum, that decision is made as part of the IEP process. Thus, if a student has some adapted curriculum goals, this curriculum modification is actually listed in the IEP accommodations section, and the student's IEP includes goals for each goal area in which the student qualifies to receive special education. Many helpful resources are available that are designed to assist IEP teams in developing IEPs that meet students' individual needs while also being appropriate for an inclusive setting (e.g., Giangreco, Cloninger, & Iverson, 1998). Prior to developing the IEP itself, many teams use a person-centered planning process (Mount & Zwernick, 1988; Vandercook, York, & Forest, 1989) to help them to determine an age-appropriate, comprehensive, yet manageable set of annual learning goals for a student. However, teachers still must determine the specific lessons in which those IEP goals will be taught and the ways that any individualized goals will be met within the context of the inclusive classroom.

Making a distinction among these three approaches to modifying curriculum goals— supplementary, simplified, and alternative— can aid the lesson planning and adaptation process in several ways. First, the use of this terminology can help team members to communicate about the ways they approach curriculum goals for individual students. Knowing whether a student's goals in a particular course or subject area will be supplemented, simplified, or altered can help to clarify the relationship between the student's learning goals and those of her or his classmates. However—and this is a very important point—this does not mean that all students should be tracked into one particular type of curriculum adaptation. The type of curriculum adaptation required may vary by subject or skill area and may also vary depending on factors such as the student's age (i.e., as students get older, their curriculum goals are often altered rather than simplified) and interests (e.g., high-interest subjects may require fewer adaptations). Adaptations may change depending on the subject area or part of the day as well. However, it may be that one type of curriculum adaptation is most suitable for a particular student at a particular point in time. For example, Sam's ninth-grade IEP team has decided that as Sam nears graduation, he will continue to participate in simplified content area instruction but will spend increasing amounts of time in vocational settings. Therefore, his IEP goals will reflect more functional applications of his academic skills.

Second, the distinction among these three ways to adapt curriculum helps IEP teams to ensure that adaptations are only as special as necessary and that students are gaining as much access as possible to the general education curriculum and age-appropriate activities and experiences. Again, the decision about a given student's instructional goals actually occurs as part of the IEP process. Thus, for the most part, students' instructional goals will already have been determined prior to the point at which a teaching team plans instructional activities and adaptations. In Chapter 4, we present a variety of assessment tools and planning formats, with suggestions about the types of curriculum adaptation for which they tend to be most useful.

Student Snapshot

 Melanie's curricular adaptations involve a combination of simplified objectives in math and language arts as well as altered, functional objectives in the areas of school routines, self-help, and communication. Therefore, at some times during the day, Melanie works on the same types of goals as her classmates, although at a different level. For example, when her classmates are using the writing process to write book reports, Melanie might write a brief book report on the computer by completing a writing frame developed by the special education teacher. Or if students are working in cooperative learning groups, Melanie may be focusing on the communication, social, and self-management skills that will enable her to function more independently in her school and community. If the group work continues for longer than Melanie is able to effectively participate, she might then use the computer to write a note about her school day for her take-home journal. Melanie also takes several movement breaks and has opportunities to use self-calming strategies when necessary to lower her frustration level and to help her to stay focused.

Instructional Adaptations: Individualizing the Methods and Materials

Instructional adaptations involve changing the way in which the teacher teaches and/or the way the student practices or demonstrates learning. That is, you may change one or more aspects of the instructional stimulus (the input) or change one or more aspects of the student response (the output) (see Table 3.4). This distinction between instructional stimulus and student response is yet another means of keeping adaptations only as special as necessary while still facilitating social and instructional participation by the student.

Adapting the Instructional Stimulus or Input

The concept of *instructional stimulus* is used very broadly here to refer to the content of the information provided during a lesson, the way in which the content is delivered, the directions and materials provided for a student during a practice or evaluation activity, and even the setting that is provided for the student. The instructional stimulus includes the content and level of difficulty and also the means by which the information is provided. For example, during a unit on reptiles, instructional stimuli might include a lecture, a textbook chapter, and oral directions for how to complete a research project. The nature and complexity of the material, the readability of the books, and the clarity of the lecture and directions are all aspects of the instructional stimuli.

Following are some examples of the ways the instructional stimulus or input can be adapted:

- In oral presentations, use controlled vocabulary and omit extraneous detail.
- Rewrite text passages, test directions, and test items at a lower readability level.
- Provide more cues, prompts, and feedback as a student completes practice activities.
- Lecture in brief, 10-minute intervals.
- Read text aloud to students.
- Accompany oral information with overheads, graphic organizers, maps, or outlines.
- Provide models and demonstrations.
- For each textbook chapter for a content area class, provide a study guide of key concepts and vocabulary terms.
- Provide audio- or videotapes to accompany textbooks.
- Conduct role plays and simulations.
- Highlight a content area textbook—yellow for vocabulary words, blue for definitions.
- Provide large-print materials, or make photocopied enlargements of written materials.
- Add pictures or symbols to text.

Adapting the Student Response or Output

The *student response*, or output, is the task that is required of the student. The student response might be listening to a lecture and taking notes, orally answering questions about a videotape, reading a textbook chapter, writing an essay, computing the answers to word problems, constructing a clay pot, or preparing a snack. For example, in a unit on reptiles, student responses might include listening to a lecture, reading resource books, taking notes, organizing and writing information in an outline format, and taking a multiple-choice test. Some examples of adaptations to the student response include the following:

Table 3.4.   Types of instructional adaptations

Type	How it's done
Instructional stimulus or input	Alter the difficulty, amount, modality, format, and/or materials used to teach
Student response or output	Alter the difficulty, amount, modality, format, and/or materials required from the student

- Complete only the two-digit multiplication problems on a page of two- and three-digit problems.

- Circle numerals named by the teacher rather than computing the problems on a math assignment.

- Work only the odd-numbered word problems on a homework assignment.

- Take notes during a lecture using a slot-note format (see Figure 5.6).

- Complete only selected steps of an art or science project.

- Use picture cues or an audiotape with the steps for completing a multistep task (e.g., a laboratory experiment, a job task)

- Give oral rather than written responses to reading comprehension questions (or vice versa).

- Use an electronic communicator rather than spelling words orally.

- Solve functional math problems rather than practicing isolated skills (e.g., hand out pencils to classmates rather than counting plastic counters to demonstrate one-to-one correspondence).

- Complete a chart, map, or outline instead of writing an essay about a novel.

In a given instructional activity, one or more aspects of the instructional stimulus, one or more aspects of the student response, or aspects of both can be adapted. For example, a student who has difficulties with focus and attention may need math worksheets with fewer problems and more white space on each page as well as a quiet place to work in order to eliminate distractions (adaptations of the instructional stimulus). A student with mental retardation may need a math worksheet that has simpler problems written in larger type (adaptation of the instructional stimulus). These students' specific needs could also be accommodated by using math cubes or other manipulatives or by having the students indicate the correct number by circling one of three numerals written by

the teacher on the worksheet (adaptations of the student response).

Choosing Appropriate Instructional Adaptations

This distinction between adaptations to the instructional stimulus and adaptations to the student response provides teachers with another way to keep adaptations only as special as necessary. Although the intrusiveness of a particular adaptation will sometimes depend on the student and the situation, some adaptations clearly are more intrusive than others. In general, adapting what the teacher does is less intrusive than adapting what the student does. If the teacher adapts the instructional stimulus by giving clearer directions, using visuals, and providing large-print materials, this is less intrusive than adapting the student response by having one student complete individually adapted materials or an altogether different activity. Likewise, if a teacher reads the directions on a math test aloud to the entire class, the test directions do not have to be written at a lower readability level for particular students. Remember that any IEP accommodations that the student should receive are prerequisites for this model. Thus, if a student's IEP requires providing materials in braille, then a braille science textbook is not considered to be an instructional adaptation that should follow the "only as special as necessary" guideline. Instead, the braille textbook is an IEP accommodation that is required in order for the student to have access to a FAPE in the LRE.

The addition of personal support or physical assistance for the student is a particular instructional adaptation that requires several cautions. Although adding the help of a teacher or paraprofessional is often the first possible adaptation that comes to mind, decisions about when and how to provide additional personal support should be part of the systematic planning of adaptations that is done by a student's core planning team. The following are some guidelines for using additional personal support wisely:

- When possible and appropriate, consider providing peer rather than adult support. Make peer helping a normal practice in the classroom, not a practice that is reserved only for students with IEPs.

- Follow the "only as special as necessary" guideline for adaptations: Provide personal support only for activities, or steps of activities, for which it is absolutely necessary.

- When adult support is provided, establish the student's participation in the activity, and then fade back the assistance until support is needed again. As teachers experienced with inclusion suggest, "Set it up and then back off."

Alternative Adaptations: Individualizing the Goal, the Instruction, and the Activity

The third category of adaptations, *alternative adaptations*, includes activities that are uniquely designed for a student with an IEP and are provided as a supplement to participation in ongoing classroom activities (see Table 3.5). In this category of adaptation, we include 1) alternative (sometimes called *parallel*) activities that are conducted in the classroom; 2) individualized instruction in fundamental IEP goals (which may occur in the classroom or elsewhere and either as one-to-one activities or in small groups); and 3) instruction in functional skill routines (which may take place inside or outside of the classroom, either in the school or in the community).

We urge you to be very judicious in the use of alternative adaptations, as they can be the most intrusive of adaptations and a hindrance to the student's inclusion in the classroom community. Alternative adaptations should be truly specialized, and they should be designed and delivered so as to be as non-stigmatizing as possible. The intent is for alternative adaptations to occur in addition to partial participation in instructional activities that occurs in the general class, not as a replacement for participation in general class activities. In many cases, a student might complete a portion or segment of a class activity and then receive alternative instruction that is needed in order to accomplish IEP goals. Another way to make alternative, out-of-class, or parallel activities acceptable is for all students in the classroom to be grouped and regrouped throughout the day and to move into and out of the classroom with teachers, volunteers, specialists, and peer tutors, either individually, in pairs, or in small groups.

In spite of these caveats, there are situations in which an IEP team may believe it necessary to provide alternative adaptations for a student with significant learning or behavioral needs. These situations arise for a variety of reasons, some of which are more educationally valid than others. It can be difficult to design adaptations that will engage a student who has significant needs for physical or behavioral support for the full duration of an extended activity, such as during a writer's workshop block or a lengthy lecture in a middle or high school class. In some cases, a spe-

Table 3.5.   Types of alternative/corresponding adaptations

Type	Characteristics
Alternative/parallel activities	Done in normative ways, with peers if possible Matches classroom themes May be part of a plan for behavioral support
Remedial or compensatory instruction	Instruction in basic skills (reading, writing, math) and individualized goals (motor skills, speech, communication)
Functional skill instruction	Instruction in functional skill routines at school and in the community Vocational instruction

What the Research Says

Pugach and Wessen (1995) interviewed students with and without learning disabilities in two fifth-grade classrooms that were taught by a general education teacher and a special education teacher. The special education teacher often provided instruction to small groups of three or four students. To avoid a group being viewed as "permanently skill deficient," groups were determined weekly and included any student who needed work on specific skills or concepts, especially in spelling and math. "Students [with learning disabilities] did not see their being taken out of the regular classroom for assistance on an ad hoc basis as problematic, in contrast to these students' dislike of formal, permanently established groups that met in resource rooms in prior years" (p. 279).

Figure 3.3.   Students' views of pull-out services.

cialist may provide alternative instruction in developmental or remedial reading or math through structured one-to-one or small-group intervention (see Figure 3.3). The least educationally valid reason for using alternative adaptations occurs when the team simply has not yet figured out a less intrusive way to make an adaptation. In such a case, further problem solving at a team meeting, perhaps involving peers or an outside consultant, is warranted.

The following are examples of alternative adaptations utilized for three of the case-study students:

- After participating in the first half of the writer's workshop, Melanie selects one activity from the "Writer's Workshop Supplementary Activity Bin."

- Vanessa, a middle school student, participates with two other students in a direct instruction, prescriptive reading program for 15 minutes each day while her classmates do silent reading in their English block. The lesson takes place in the library and is taught by a special education teacher.

- Walter, an eleventh grader, works for 1.5 hours per day at a pizza restaurant where he will be employed during the summer and possibly after graduation.

When alternative adaptations are used, it is important to ask these questions:

1. Is the problem that you have not yet figured out a less intrusive adaptation?

2. Is the activity as brief as possible and well timed to match natural breaks in the classroom schedule?

3. Are peers included whenever possible?

4. Is the alternative adaptation coordinated with classroom content and themes?

5. Does the alternative activity provide intensive instruction in pivotal IEP goals?

6. Is it the norm for all students in the classroom to be grouped and regrouped throughout the day and moving into and out of the classroom?

Additional Considerations for Students with Serious Behavior Problems

Many of the strategies that may be used to support students with disabilities who have serious behavior problems might be considered to be instructional adaptations or alternative adaptations. For example, scheduling academic work in smaller chunks of time, providing preferential seating, and limiting the size of the groups in which a student participates could all be considered instructional adaptations. Providing a place to go to calm down and adding more active, functional out-of-class activities to the student's schedule could be considered alternative adaptations.

These and other adaptations that are used as part of behavioral support plans are examined in *Behavioral Support* (Janney & Snell, 2000), another volume in the *Teachers' Guides to Inclusive Practices* series.

STAGES OF CREATING ADAPTATIONS

One challenge that teachers may encounter in creating individualized adaptations is finding ways to plan ahead so that they are not always "winging it." One helpful strategy is to break the process down into two stages (see Table 3.6). In the first stage, the team determines which adaptations can be planned for and used for an extended period of time. This first stage involves creating *general adaptations*. Next, adaptations that are required for specific lessons or activities can be designed on a weekly or daily basis. These *specific adaptations* are unique, time-limited adaptations designed for a particular lesson, activity, or unit.

General Adaptations

General adaptations are based on the assumption that most classrooms operate according to somewhat predictable patterns. Teachers tend to have an established schedule of daily routines, to use a particular subset of instructional strategies and approaches repeatedly, and to give students certain types of assignments or tasks. Because of these pre-dictable patterns, lessons and activities often can be adapted in similar ways for a period of time. These are *general adaptations*, patterns or formats for adapting the predictable routines and instructional designs used in the classroom. (Some special education teachers prefer to call these *global adaptations;* others might use the term *routine adaptations*.) They can be planned in advance and used repeatedly.

For example, in elementary classrooms, a typical daily morning routine includes putting away belongings, making lunch choices, saying the pledge of allegiance, and so forth. During this time, Daniel, the first-grade student with multiple disabilities, puts away his belongings with physical support from an instructional assistant. Next, the class does the letter-of-the-day routine, which involves identifying a letter of the alphabet, naming things that start with that letter, and then copying the letter and words on paper. Daniel's task is to use a rubber name stamp to identify his daily letter sheet and to color a picture of an object that begins with that letter. Following the letter-of-the-day routine, students write a daily journal entry based on a writing prompt that the teacher has written on the chalkboard. During journal writing, another predictable activity, Daniel uses an electronic communicator to choose a classmate to assist him with cutting and pasting a picture in his journal. This classmate records a comment about the picture into Daniel's communicator so that Daniel can play it back during share time later in the morning.

During this sequence of morning activities, Daniel's curricular goals (putting away his belongings, using his name stamp, and

Table 3.6. Stages of creating adaptations

Stage	Characteristics
1. General adaptations	Blueprints or formats for adapting predictable activities and routines Typical adaptations to goals, methods, materials, and personal support
2. Specific adaptations	Time-limited adaptation for a particular, specific lesson, activity, or unit Matches class content and activity

using his electronic communication system) are predictable. The instructional adaptations, which include the physical positioning strategy and the prompting routine used by the assistant and most of the adapted materials for his journal entry, also remain the same from day to day. All of these general adaptations have been planned by Daniel's team and are described in Classroom Participation Plans with General Adaptations (described in Chapter 4), which were written by Cyndi Pitonyak, the special education teacher.

General adaptations may also be developed in middle or high school for subjects or courses in which certain instructional formats and activities are used consistently. For example, in Sam's ninth-grade world geography class, the teacher, Mr. Sailor, often begins the lesson with a lecture, which typically includes demonstrations and practice in using map-reading skills. For each lecture, Sam uses a daily note sheet that has been prepared to reflect his simplified goals for the course (he learns only selected, key concepts and map skills for each unit of study) and his limited note-taking ability. Once or twice per week, Mr. Sailor asks students to volunteer to read aloud from the textbook. At these times, no adaptations are needed for Sam, who simply does not read aloud unless he chooses to. Twice per week, typically, Mr. Sailor assigns approximately 20 minutes of individual seatwork, which may include answering chapter questions, looking up vocabulary words, or completing map worksheets. The general adaptation provided for Sam is extra prompting and monitoring (by the classroom assistant or Mr. Sailor) and reminders to refer to the appropriate data sources when answering questions. On the other 3 days of the week, the remainder of the class period is spent with the students working on research projects in cooperative groups. Because Sam has difficulties interacting with peers, he is placed with a particular group of classmates who know him well whenever cooperative group work is assigned.

The general ways that each of these predictable activities will be adapted for Sam were determined at the beginning of the se-

mester. The general adaptations for Sam's world geography class include 1) the format of his daily note sheet, 2) the extra prompting and monitoring from the assistant or teacher during seatwork, and 3) placing Sam with particular peers for the cooperative activity. The content of general adaptations, such as Sam's daily note sheet and his specific contributions to the cooperative group project, must reflect the week's specific topic; however, the general format for how the class activities are adapted for Sam remains constant for some time.

Once general adaptations, such as those described, have been designed for Daniel and Sam, the same general adaptation "blueprints" can be used repeatedly. Planning for these general adaptations requires knowledge of classroom routines, instructional formats, and student goals and support needs. However, once designed and communicated to the team, many general adaptations can be implemented with minimal day-to-day planning.

Specific Adaptations

Although general adaptations can be designed for these predictable classroom routines and instructional formats, the specific curriculum objectives addressed change daily, weekly, or monthly. This means that adaptations that relate to specific content or skills need to vary accordingly. Also, some adaptations may vary because they are required during a new activity or during an activity that is only performed periodically.

Adaptations that must vary according to lesson content or structure are called *specific adaptations*. In contrast with general adaptations, specific adaptations may require short-term planning between the classroom teacher and special education staff. For example, the pictures that Daniel colors on his letter-of-the-day page are of objects that begin with the particular letter that the class is studying. If Tuesday's letter is *r*, Daniel col-

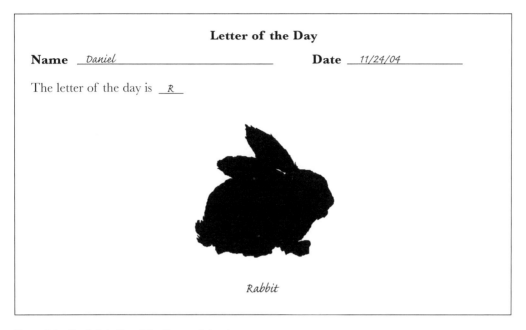

Figure 3.4. Daniel's Letter-of-the-Day worksheet.

ors a picture of a rabbit that the assistant has found and photocopied onto Daniel's letter-of-the-day worksheet. Daniel's classroom teacher and special education teacher (or assistant) need to share information about the morning letter because special education support staff have agreed to be responsible for preparing the appropriate pictures for Daniel to color (see Figure 3.4).

In Sam's world geography class, although the teacher uses a fairly routine set of activities for most class sessions, the topic of the lessons varies from week to week. Therefore, the specific content that Sam learns varies according to the class unit topic. One week, it may be regions of the African desert; the next week, it might be how mountains are formed. Making content-related adaptations requires weekly communication and joint planning between the world geography teacher and the special education teacher. They must discuss the lesson content so that Sam's note sheet and his contribution to the cooperative group project can be prepared.

Why Distinguish Between General and Specific Adaptations?

The distinction between general and specific adaptations allows teachers to divide the planning into two stages: The first stage focuses on getting general adaptations into place, and the second stage focuses on creating specific adaptations. Planning is also facilitated by understanding that the type of curriculum adaptation used for a student can help to predict whether the student will tend to need more general or specific adaptations. Students whose curriculum objectives are simplified versions of the general class objectives will tend to need more specific adaptations because their curriculum content varies according to the content of class lessons. In contrast, students whose curriculum objectives have been altered to a functional curriculum will tend to need more general adaptations because their curriculum content is less determined by the general education content. The specific adaptations developed for students with altered curriculum objectives primarily focus on keep-

What the Research Says

Potter (1992) studied the contrast between the ways that special education teachers and general education teachers tend to plan. She noted that general education teachers, facing large groups of students and a standardized curriculum, tend to focus more on creating tasks. That is, they select the content to cover and then plan the routines or activities in which students will be involved. In contrast, special education teachers, who deal with smaller numbers of students, tend to use a means–end planning model that begins by specifying objectives and then organizing learning activities.

Potter suggested that asking a classroom teacher to adapt to the needs of students with disabilities by creating entirely new classroom routines and instructional procedures may be overwhelming at first. Therefore, it may be best to begin by

Finding ways to incorporate the student's needs into the existing classroom routines. . . . The more quickly routines can be redeveloped, the sooner the teacher will [be able to] deal with the more complex aspects of the student's integration. Also, if a student is not included in normal classroom routines, he or she is not really part of the classroom unit and a major goal of integration is lost. (pp. 123–124)

She urged special educators to remember that the classroom teacher is more likely to plan around activities than to plan around objectives. An important function of the special educator's role is to keep the integrated student's goals and objectives in mind when planning with the classroom teacher about how activities can be adapted for the student.

Figure 3.5.   How teachers plan.

ing the student connected with the topics and themes being studied by classmates.

The routine nature of many classroom activities makes developing adaptations a bit less demanding than if the class schedule and the way teachers teach varies extensively from day to day. An approach to making adaptations that take advantage of this aspect of classroom life also fits with classroom teachers' approach to planning because they tend to plan in terms of content and activities, rather than planning from individualized objectives as special educators are taught to do (see Figure 3.5). The planning processes suggested in Chapter 4 build on this concept.

EVALUATING THE "SPECIALNESS" OF ADAPTATIONS

One way to evaluate the adaptations that have been developed is to check them against a list of types of adaptations organized in order from least to most special. The list provided in Table 3.7 is generally consistent with suggestions made by other educators who have

developed materials on adaptations and modifications in inclusive classrooms (e.g., Giangreco, Cloninger, & Iverson, 1998; Strickland & Turnbull, 1990; Udvari-Solner, 1994). As a general rule, adapting teacher behavior is less intrusive than adapting what the student does.

SUMMARY

The adaptations model, described in this chapter, provides a framework for thinking about which aspects of a lesson—the curricular goal and/or the instructional methods—should be adapted or whether an alternative adaptation should be provided, which alters the goal, the instruction, and the activity itself. The model also makes a distinction between two levels of planning of adaptations, with general adaptations being ongoing and specific adaptations being time-limited. The model proposes two criteria that should be met by individualized adaptations: that they result in both academic and social participation and that they be only as special as necessary.

Table 3.7.   Adaptations that are only as special as necessary

Prerequisites to the model for individualized adaptations	The classroom is truly inclusive (i.e., neighborhood schools, general and special education collaboration, inclusive culture).
	Accommodating, evidence-based teaching practices are in place.
	The student has an IEP that includes • Access to the general curriculum • IEP accommodations that enable access to a free, appropriate public education (FAPE) in the least restrictive environment (LRE)
Three types of adaptations	Alter the curriculum goals for the student. Include the student's adapted IEP goals and accommodations in initial, classwide planning. • Supplementary goals • Simplified goals • Alternative, functional goals

	Alter the methods or materials.
	• Consider changing the instructional stimulus.
	• Consider changing the student response.
	• Consider providing additional personal support
	    From peers
	    From adults

	Change to an alternative adaption that is coordinated with classroom instruction. • After or before part of the class activity • With peers • Without peers

Chapter 4

Steps for Making Individualized Adaptations

This chapter describes the steps and tools of planning individualized adaptations for students (see Figure 4.1). It is important to re-emphasize that this is a collaborative process and that adaptation strategies are generated and evolve as teams work together. The planning forms illustrated in the chapter should, of course, be adapted by teams to fit the specific needs of the students as well as the planning styles of the teachers. However, we—the authors and the teachers who contributed to this book—strongly recommend that all teachers in a school adopt a basic set of planning formats that are recognized and used schoolwide, with other team-specific or student-specific forms added as needed. This practice enhances communication among teachers in the school and also makes students' transition from one grade level to the next more seamless.

Although the process is presented in a sequence of six steps, in reality, the steps may

---

Steps and Tools for Planning Individualized Adaptations

Step 1. Gather Information

    a. About the Student

        ❏ Student Information Form (Confidential) (Figure 4.3)

        ❏ Program-at-a-Glance (Figure 4.4)

    b. About the Classroom

        ❏ General Assessment of Classroom Activities (Figure 4.5)

        {❏} Ecological Assessment of Classroom Activities (Figure 4.7)

Step 2. Determine When Adaptations Are Needed

        ❏ General Assessment of Classroom Activities (Figure 4.5)

        {❏} Program Planning Matrix (Figure 4.10)

Step 3. Decide on Planning Strategies

        ❏ Guide to Adaptation Planning Strategies (Individual) (Figure 4.11)

Step 4. Plan and Implement Adaptations: First General, Then Specific

    a. ❏ Individualized Adaptations Plan (Figure 4.12) and/or

        {❏} Classroom Participation Plan with General Adaptations (Figure 4.13)

    b. ❏ Weekly Plan for Specific Adaptations (Figure 4.14 [elementary] or Figure 4.15 [secondary])

Step 5. Plan and Implement Alternative Adaptations

Step 6. Monitor and Evaluate

        ❏ Team Meeting Agenda and Minutes (Figure 4.18)

        ❏ Team Evaluation of Student Adaptations

Key: {❏} indicates tools typically used only for students with severe disabilities. Most often, these are students who have extensive support needs and significant curricular adaptations.

Figure 4.1.   Steps and tools for planning individualized adaptations.

Table 4.1. Case studies

Student	Grade	Diagnosis	Curricular adaptations
Daniel	First	Severe disabilities	Altered (functional)
Melanie	Fourth	Autism	Simplified and altered
Vanessa	Seventh	Learning disability	Supplementary (social and self-management skills, reading)
Sam	Ninth	Emotional/behavioral disorder	Simplified and altered (in vocational domain)
Walter	Eleventh	Mental retardation	Altered (functional)

overlap or occur in a somewhat different order, depending on the circumstances. The most fundamental first step is ensuring that the student is connected with peers through a range of social interactions and that he or she is treated as a full and equal member of the classroom group.

Five students who have a range of abilities and support needs are used throughout this chapter as examples to illustrate the adaptation planning process. Table 4.1 lists the five students first introduced in Chapter 1, along with information about their grade level and the type of curriculum adaptation that tends to characterize their IEPs. Further information about these students is presented in their Programs-at-a-Glance, which are provided later in the chapter.

It is impossible to illustrate how each step of the planning process can be used for each school level and every student; therefore, these five students are used to illustrate some of the key ways in which the adaptation planning process varies across the elementary, middle, and high school ages and across varying levels of support. In addition to variations in the adaptation planning process across school/grade level, the other key factor affecting the planning methods used for these students is the type of curricular adaptation that tends to characterize their IEP goals.

Although this chapter focuses on planning adaptations for individual students, a particular team, or various members of several teams, may actually serve several students with IEPs in the same classroom. Some strategies to assist in planning for multiple students are described in *Collaborative Teaming* (Snell & Janney, 2005), another volume in the *Teachers' Guides to Inclusive Practices* series.

We caution you that the array of forms illustrated in this chapter may at first make the process seem more complex than it actually is. However, many of the forms are completed either once per year or once per semester, and some are required only for students with extensive support needs. In spite of the effort it takes to implement this process, it is important to have written documentation of decisions that have been made about the individualized adaptation process. Maintaining the integrity of students' education requires planning and evaluation, even though all teachers have to be prepared to think on their feet at times.

Step 1

Gather and Share Information About the Student and the Classroom

The first step in the individualized adaptation process is to gather and share information that will assist the classroom teacher, special education teacher, instructional assistants, and other team members to create a good fit between the student and the classroom (see Figure 4.2). This requires gathering information to assist the team in getting to know the student and getting to know the demands of the classroom. Essentially, the team needs to answer three questions:

1. What are the demands of the classroom?

2. What are the student's characteristics, educational needs, and skills?

3. What adaptations will improve the fit between the student and the classroom and also ensure belonging and achievement?

Information About the Student

What information does the team need to know about the student? In addition to knowing what instructional goals are appropriate for the student, the team also needs to have a sense of who the student is and what works for the student. As early as possible in the school year (or during the spring before, if possible), the special education service coordinator should assemble a packet of information about the student for the classroom teacher and other team members. The amount and type of information required will vary depending on the student, but a two-page, front-to-back form combining a Student Information Form and a Program-at-a-Glance will most likely be needed for each student with an IEP. These two forms are most helpful when they are part of the set of planning forms that teachers across the school have agreed to use for their students with IEPs.

Student Information Form

The Student Information Form includes information that will be helpful in determining appropriate programming for the student. The form includes a list of the student's special education and related services, medical/health information, interests, and a summary of what works and does not work with the student. It is best to share this information initially in a face-to-face meeting of the core team so that any additional questions can be asked and answered. The general education teacher keeps the Student Information Form, with only the student's initials on it, in a grade book or other convenient but private place. Figure 4.3 shows a Student Information Form for Melanie.

For students with severe disabilities and extensive support needs, the team will probably need a more comprehensive collection of biographical and educational information. A Student Notebook that includes additional information about the family, the student's IEP, instructional program plans, and evaluation tools is described as part of the monitoring and evaluation process outlined in Step 6.

Program-at-a-Glance

Although the classroom teacher and others who support the student need to be informed

---

Voices from the Classroom

Kenna Colley, a former special education consulting teacher, states that one of the keys to designing adaptations that work is to build on the things that each classroom teacher does well: "The general education teacher needs to be central in the decision making about adaptations, or you may end up planning wonderful adaptations that are not compatible with that teacher's teaching methods." For example, one teacher used "literature circles" in which small groups of students discussed each novel that was read. At first, Ms. Colley would plan alternative activities for Melanie to work on during literature circles, such as building a 3-D model to illustrate the novel. Ms. Colley saw that working on these alternative activities meant that Melanie missed out on frequent opportunities for interactions with classmates and reinforcement of the novel content. As a result, Ms. Colley instead provided the classroom teacher with suggestions about ways to enable Melanie to contribute to the literature circle discussion. The hands-on activities that she had been planning solely for Melanie were used as part of a learning center that provided students with a variety of extension activities related to the current novel.

Figure 4.2. Adaptations that work.

Student Information Form (Confidential)

Student _Melanie_   **Grade** _4_   **School Year** _2004–2005_

Current Teachers _Pitonyak and Ramirez_   **Last Year's Teachers** _Fuller and Roberts_

Special Education & Related Services ✔ Academics (list) *all areas* ✔ Speech: *20 minutes x 3 days* ✔ Occupational therapy: *20 minutes x 1 day* ___ Physical therapy: ✔ Aide support: *5 hours x 5 days* ✔ Sp. ed. instruction: *12 hours x 5 days* ✔ Sp. ed. consultation: *1 hour per week* ___ Other:	**Likes** *Picture books and magazines* *Computer for writing* *Her own space: a place for her things, room to move around* **Dislikes** *Loud noises* *Being read to without book to follow along* *Peanut butter, grape juice, catsup!* *Being confined or cramped*
Medical/health ___ Medication ___ Allergies ___ Diabetes ___ Seizures ___ Other medical/physical needs:	**See guidance counselor/ principal for other relevant confidential information?** ✔ yes ___ no **Behavior Plan?** ✔ yes (attach) ___ no **SOL Testing Accommodations?** ___ yes ___ no **Type of diploma** _to be determined_
What works/learns best when ___ Seeing (needs picture/graphic organizer) ___ Hearing and doing (teacher modeling) ___ Moving (hands-on work, labs, field trips) ___ Getting multisensory input (all of the above)	**Other important information/ areas of concern** *Communicate with both words and pictures*

Figure 4.3.   Student Information Form.

about the student's IEP, the IEP itself tends to be too cumbersome to be used for ongoing team planning regarding adaptations. The Program-at-a-Glance is a communication tool designed to give the classroom teacher and others who work with a student a quick overview of the student's educational program. Usually completed by the special education teacher, it includes a brief list of IEP goals and accommodations. It also provides information about the student's academic or social management needs, including references to behavior management plans and eating, positioning, or toileting needs. The Program-at-a-Glance can be provided on the back of the Student Information Form. Figure 4.4 shows a Program-at-a-Glance for Melanie.

Program-at-a-Glance	
Student _____ Melanie _____	**Date** __ 10/2004 __
IEP goals	**IEP accommodations**
Social/communication • *Use devices/systems to express needs and feelings, ask questions, make choices, express yes/no, greet people* • *Use gestures consistently* • *Relate recent events in two- or three-word sentences* Functional skills • *Follow task directions from cues* • *School arrival, departure, lunch routines* • *School/classroom jobs* Math • *Identify numbers 0–1,000* • *Number line for less than, more than* • *Time to minute (face, digit)* Language arts • *Comprehension questions, novels* • *Computer journal writing* • *Read/write/spell functional words* • *Inventive spelling for class assignments* Content areas • *Key words/concepts for each unit*	• *Receive special education assistance/ instruction with academics, daily routines, transitions, support for communication techniques, peer interactions* • *Weekly curricular adaptations by special ed. and general ed. teachers* • *Designated location in school for breaks* • *Home–school communication log* • *Educational team familiar with and uses all augmentative communication methods* • *Behavior intervention plan to teach relaxation and self-calming*
Academic/ social management needs	**Comments/special needs**
• *Peer planning at beginning of the year and as needed* • *Reduced information per page* • *Checklists and graphic organizers for time limits and beginnings/endings*	• *Anecdotal records for IEP progress* • *Core team meetings weekly; whole team meetings monthly* • *Share autism info. with all team members and relevant staff*

Figure 4.4.   Program-at-a-Glance for Melanie.

Information About the Classroom

In order for the student to be meaningfully included, his or her team needs to know certain information about the classroom; it is important to understand the classroom's typical rules and routines, the way the teacher teaches, and the ways the students interact. Each classroom has its own unique structure and climate, both of which should be reflected in the student's plan for adaptations.

General Assessment of Classroom Activities

To know when adaptations are required, the team needs to assess the classroom, including its structure, routines, types of instructional activities, curriculum, and climate. The extent and detail of information needed varies greatly, depending on the student's age and support needs. For students with mild disabilities who participate in the general education curriculum with only intermittent support, an informal, global appraisal of the demands of the classroom and the students' abilities is often adequate. That is, given that the teacher or teachers know the student and the student's IEP relatively well, the team can easily identify significant discrepancies among the student's current capabilities and those required for full participation in the classroom. For example, Vanessa, who has a learning disability, can easily comprehend sophisticated academic material that is read to her. However, she is not able to read the material fast enough to complete in-class reading assignments and requires more than the allotted time to complete homework that involves reading. A formal observation of Vanessa's performance in each of her academic classes is not necessary for her teachers to know that she will require some adaptations and accommodations in any class that requires more than two or three pages of reading per day.

Designing effective adaptations for students who have simplified or alternate curriculum goals, however, will at times require gathering more detailed information about things such as typical instructional formats and procedures, types of in-class and homework assignments, testing formats and types of tests, and classroom rules and expectations. A General Assessment of Classroom Activities is conducted by the special education teacher through classroom observations and an interview with the classroom teacher during the first few weeks of the school year or semester. This information is used both to identify when adaptations are needed and to provide support personnel, including assistants and related service providers, with information about the classroom. As with other aspects of the adaptation process, this assessment is performed for each class period for both middle schools and high schools. In elementary schools, the daily classroom schedule usually reflects activities for each subject area and is divided into morning and afternoon sections; therefore, the assessment strategies and the development of adaptation plans would follow that formula.

Figure 4.5 is an Assessment of Classroom Activities for Sam's ninth-grade world geography class. (Sam's Program-at-a-Glance is provided in Figure 4.6.) In the first section of the form, "Instructional Activities," the two teachers have listed the typical instructional activities and frequently used student responses or tasks. In this class, the teacher uses whole-class activities (e.g., lectures, discussions, films), small cooperative group projects, and independent activities (e.g., textbook reading, seatwork). In the "Adaptations?" column of this section, the special education teacher has made notes that will help guide the remaining steps of the process—determining whether Sam can perform the particular activity as it stands or whether adaptations are needed. Also described on the form are the homework requirements for the class, the textbooks and other frequently used materials, the amount and types of assistance that the general education teacher provides for students, and the testing formats and procedures. In the final section of the form, the classroom rules and norms for behavior are described. The special education teacher has also indicated whether Sam will need individualized adaptations for each of these types of classroom procedures.

General Assessment of Classroom Activities

Subject/Grade Level _World Geography/9th_   **Date** _9/2004_

Student _Sam_   **Teacher** _Sailor_

Instructional Activities		
Typical activities	**Frequently used student responses/tasks**	**Adaptations?**
Whole class		
• Lecture/discussion	• Take notes from board and overhead projector; raise hands to volunteer answers to questions (daily)	Yes
• Maps	• Locate places, describe/discuss geographic features (almost daily)	No
• Films	• Take notes, discuss (≈1 time per week)	No
• Oral reading of text	• students volunteer to read (2–3 times per week)	No
Small groups		
• Cooperative projects	• Research, writing reports in groups of 4 (1–2 times/week)	Yes (minimal)
Independent		
• Silent reading	• (1–2 times per week)	Yes
• Seatwork	• Answer chapter questions, look up vocabulary words, map worksheets (2–3 times per week)	Yes
Homework (frequency and approximate duration) Mon.–Thurs., 20–30 minutes; usually have a few minutes at end of period to start		Yes
Textbooks, other frequently used materials		
• World Geography text		Yes
• Atlas, globe, wall maps		No
General education teacher assistance Teacher circulates throughout room, providing many opportunities to ask questions; checks frequently for understanding. Students are encouraged to ask each other.		Yes
Evaluation/testing Test/quiz format • Unit tests: multiple choice, matching, true/false • Vocabulary quiz for each unit: fill in the blank Sources of information for tests • Textbook, lecture notes, worksheets • Review 1 day prior to test: good opportunity for students to prepare study guide		Yes to all (As per IEP)
Classroom rules and contingencies • Must bring textbook, paper, pencil • Strict enforcement of school conduct code re: attendance, language, etc. • Students must make up all missed work within 2 days of absence for credit **Norms for student interaction and movement** • Raise hand during lecture/discussion; talking okay while working in groups • May move around to sharpen pencils, get atlases, etc., except during lecture or test **Procedures for routines** • student at front of each row hands out/collects papers • Folder on teacher's desk with previous day's handouts for students who were absent		Yes to all (As per IEP)

Figure 4.5.   General assessment of classroom activities. (Contributed by Johnna Elliott.)

Program-at-a-Glance

Student _____ Sam _____ **Date** _ 10/2004 _____

IEP goals	**IEP accommodations**

IEP goals

Social/behavioral and self-management
- *Identify triggers for anxiety; read social stories to prepare for identified trigger situations; use relaxation and self-calming strategies with prompts*
- *Maintain appropriate topics of conversation with peers and adults*
- *Maintain agenda with daily/weekly schedule, homework assignments, plans for long-term project*

English
- *Locate information with a reference source*
- *Listen to literature selections and answer literal and inferential comprehension questions*
- *Use writing process to compose stories and essays with appropriate paragraph structure and sequence, spelling, punctuation*

Vocational goals
- *Identify job interests*
- *Job exploration in four targeted areas of interest*
- *Follow written and verbal task directions for arrival and departure from job site, job tasks, and break routine*

Math
- *Use calculator for computations in functional school, work, and community contexts*

World Geography
- *Key words/concepts for each unit of study*
- *Define and use selected terms related to geographical features, map symbols*

IEP accommodations
- *Receive special education assistance/ instruction with English, World Geography, work–study; monitor transitions, cafeteria, PE, food service*
- *Receive prompts for use of daily agenda and organizational tools required for specific classes*
- *Weekly curricular adaptations by special ed. and general ed. teachers for English, World Geography*
- *Designated location in school for breaks*
- *Positive behavioral support plan inservice for Sam's teachers and assistants*
- *Intervention plan to teach relaxation and self-calming*

Academic/ social management needs
- *Peer planning at beginning of the year and as needed*
- *Checklists and graphic organizers for assignments/projects that extend over multiple days/tasks*

Comments/special needs
- *Anecdotal records for IEP progress*
- *Whole team meetings monthly for IEP and behavior support plan evaluation*
- *share obsessive-compulsive disorder information with all team members and relevant staff*

Figure 4.6.   Program-at-a-Glance for Sam.

Ecological Assessment of Classroom Activities

For students with more extensive support needs whose curricular goals are significantly altered to include functional skills and/or embedded motor, social, and communication skills, the assessment of the classroom will include more detailed descriptions of the steps of each type of instructional activity and will require actual observations of the student's classroom performance. This assessment involves a step-by-step listing of the typical steps and procedures for each class activity or routine. It also includes an assessment of the student's current participation in each step. Using this information, the team then identifies skills needed by the student and individualized adaptations that could be provided to increase the student's participation.

For example, Figure 4.7 shows part of an Ecological Assessment of Classroom Activities for the calendar math routine that is conducted daily in Daniel's classroom. (Figure 4.8 shows Daniel's Program-at-a-Glance.) Daniel's teachers first listed all of the subjects scheduled across the day (e.g., reading, language arts, math, art, music, physical education) and the typical activities that were used within each subject area. For math, the typical activities included number games and worksheets, counting centers, and calendar math. As shown in Figure 4.7, Daniel's special education teacher observed the calendar math activity and wrote down a description of the typical sequence of steps and procedures, in addition to what Daniel actually did during each step and whether the assistant supported him at the time. The Ecological Assessment of Classroom Activities can be used both to help determine IEP goals for a student within the "classroom participation" domain and to analyze the need for adaptations to enable the student to participate more fully in ongoing classroom activities.

Thus, for students such as Daniel, the process for assessing the classroom is essentially the same as the ecological assessment process that is used to develop an individualized, community-referenced instructional program for students who require instruction in functional skills for daily living. However, this particular ecological assessment is conducted within the classroom, rather than within one of the other community-living environments in which the student may be receiving instruction. (For more information on the ecological assessment process and using it to develop a community-referenced IEP, see Ford et al., 1989; Giangreco, Cloninger, & Iverson, 1998; Snell & Brown, 2000.)

Step 2

Determine When Adaptations Are Needed

The next step in the process is to determine specifically when adaptations are needed. This step varies significantly, depending on how the student's curriculum goals are modified.

For Students with Supplementary Curriculum Goals

Vanessa's IEP consists primarily of supplementary curriculum goals to improve her reading, study, and organizational skills, along with accommodations for in-class reading assignments and test-taking. Very few unique adaptations are required in order for her to participate in her middle school courses. For a student like Vanessa, most of the information about when she will require accommodations and adaptations is already included on the Program-at-a-Glance (see Figure 4.9). For example, Vanessa's social studies class occasionally requires in-class reading assignments that she is not able to complete in the allotted time. Therefore, one of her IEP accommodations is that social studies reading assignments may be read aloud to her (by a peer or instructional assistant) during study hall. In English, books on tape of the literature selections are provided so that Vanessa can listen to them at home or during study hall. Other than ordering the books on tape

Ecological Assessment of Classroom Activities

Teacher ___James___ **Grade** _1_ **Student** ___Daniel___
Subject _Math_ **Activity** _Calendar math_ **Time** _12:15–12:35_ **Date** _9/22/04_

Typical sequence of steps/procedures	Target student participation
1. Teacher calls for attention and tells students to sit on the floor in front of the room.	1. Full physical assistance from assistant to walk to front and sit on the floor. Other students are seated and the teacher has begun by the time Daniel is seated.
2. Teacher points to date chart. Students respond orally as she asks for yesterday's date, today's date, number of days of school left yesterday and today, and whether today's number is bigger or smaller.	2. Assistant positions Daniel on the floor and provides hip support. Daniel attends to the teacher.
3. Teacher calls on one student to tell today's weather and makes a tally mark beside the weather symbol. She asks for the number of days they have had that weather. Students count tallies by 5s and 1s.	3. Assistant cues Daniel by saying "Let's clap" when the teacher asks students to count aloud. He claps the assistant's hand as she counts aloud in Daniel's ear.
4. Teacher: "Yesterday was [she names day of the week]. Today is [students name day of the week]." Students and teacher spell out the day of the week while clapping for each letter. Then, two or three students are called on to spell the day and clap independently.	4. Assistant cues Daniel: "Let's clap [number of letters in the day of the week]." Daniel claps her palm as she counts aloud in his ear, then grasps his hand to signal "stop."
5. Teacher points to strings of beads labeled 100s, 10s, and 1s and adds one more. She calls on one student to count the beads, then another to say the number.	5. Daniel attends to teacher.
6. Teacher: "Let's count." All count by 10s and 1s to day of the school year.	6. Daniel's head drops and assistant repositions herself.

Skills needed to increase participation

1. Raise hand to signal the teacher for an opportunity to respond.
2. Count by 1s and 10s (by clapping another person's hand).
3. Answer yes/no questions using a switch.

Adaptations needed to increase participation

1. Get to front of room sooner—carry him or start sooner?
2. Yes/no switchplate

Figure 4.7. Ecological Assessment of Classroom Activities. (Contributed by Johnna Elliot.)

Program-at-a-Glance

Student _____ _Daniel_ _____   **Date** ___ _10/2004_ ___

IEP goals	**IEP accommodations**
Social/behavioral and self-management	• *Receive special education assistance/ instruction with academics, daily routines, transitions, support for communication techniques and peer interaction*
• *Use simple switches and picture symbols to make choices among 2–3 items or activities*	• *Adapted curriculum emphasizing functional skills, social/communication, and participation in ongoing class routines and activities*
• *Attend to classmates during small group activities*	• *Home–school communication log*
• *Raise hand, use switch to relate events in two- or three-word sentences*	• *Educational team familiar with and uses all augmentative communication methods*
Functional skills	• *Variety of manipulatives for math activities*
• *Use a picture schedule with minimal prompts to indicate the next activity and termination of the current activity*	• *Weekly coplanning to determine adaptations for participation in language arts and math activities*
• *Increase independence in school arrival, departure, and lunch routines as per program plans*	
• *School/classroom jobs with peer partner*	
Math	
• *Identify numbers 1–10*	
• *Count objects to 10 in math activities and in functional contexts throughout the day*	
Language arts	
• *Identify name in print*	
• *Cut/color/paste pictures and words for language activities*	
• *Participate in selected steps of cooperative group reading, writing, and word study projects/activities*	
Classroom participation	
• *Participate in at least half of all ongoing classroom routines and activities*	
Academic/ social management needs	**Comments/special needs**
• *Peer planning and problem solving at beginning of year and as needed*	• *Anecdotal records and skill acquisition data for IEP progress*
• *Special education aide support for math and arrival, lunch, departure, and bathroom routines*	• *Core team meetings weekly; whole team meetings monthly*
• *Position close to classmates in variety of suitable positions as per PT/OT plans*	• *Pull-in occupational therapy (OT), physical therapy (PT), and speech-language therapy services. Pull-out PT for 30 min. once per 6 weeks to evaluate movement and equipment*

Figure 4.8.   Program-at-a-Glance for Daniel.

Program-at-a-Glance

Student _____ Vanessa _____   **Date** ___ 10/2004 ___

IEP goals	**IEP accommodations**
Reading • *Improve word recognition and fluency through individualized reading program during study hall/resource period* English • *Use writing process to write essays, reports, and fiction* Organization and self-management (all classes) • *Maintain agenda with daily/weekly schedule, homework assignments, plans for long-term projects*	• *May have access to lecture notes, study guides, or models (social studies, English)* • *Social studies text read aloud to her during study hall/resource period* • *Extra time on tests and written assignments as needed, as long as reasonable progress is shown and extra time is negotiated beforehand* • *Books on tape provided for English* • *Oral testing on essay questions for elaboration of written responses, if needed*
Academic/ social management needs	**Comments/special needs**
• *Significant discrepancy between ability and written language skills* • *Reading and writing are very slow, but she recalls information and grasps abstract concepts easily*	• *Excellent general knowledge and comprehension*

Figure 4.9. Program-at-a-Glance for Vanessa.

ahead of time so that they will be available to Vanessa as needed, little planning is required to provide her accommodations.

For Students with Simplified Curriculum Goals

For students who have simplified curriculum goals in a particular subject or goal area, the determination of when adaptations are needed can be made directly from the Assessment of Classroom Activities and Procedures. That is, the teacher or teachers, given that they know the student and the student's IEP relatively well, can simply note in the right-hand column on the General Assess-

ment of Classroom Activities whether each task or activity needs to be adapted. For example, as indicated on the assessment of Sam's world geography class (see Figure 4.5), Sam needs adaptations during lectures and discussions, small-group cooperative projects, and seatwork; however, he can participate independently during map reading, watching films, and oral reading from the text. He also needs adaptations to homework and tests.

For Students with Altered Curriculum Goals

If a student's curricular goals are significantly different from those of his or her classmates, the student's adaptation plan must indicate how the student's goals dovetail with those of other students. The *curriculum matrix* is a planning tool that has been used by various authors for several different purposes in a variety of forms. (It was first published in an earlier edition of Giangreco, Cloninger, and Iverson's *Choosing Outcomes and Accommodations for Children [COACH]: A Guide to Educational Planning for Students with Disabilities* [1998].)

Program Planning Matrix

When the curriculum is altered to include functional and/or embedded skills, another step is required to determine when adaptations are needed. First, the student's team must know when and where the student's individualized goals will be taught. The Program Planning Matrix helps them to analyze which altered curriculum goals will be addressed in each class activity. The Program Planning Matrix is completed by the core team, with the guidance of the special education teacher, as early in the school year as possible. As shown in Figure 4.10, the student's IEP goals are listed in the left-hand column, and the class activity schedule is listed across the top row. An "x" in a cell indicates the IEP goals that will be addressed during the corresponding class activities.

Melanie's IEP goals include simplified academic goals as well as alternate goals for functional skill routines and embedded social-communication skills. Using the matrix is a straightforward process for the parts of Melanie's day during which her simplified academic goals are addressed. Melanie's reading and writing goals are addressed during the class journal writing activity, the language arts block, and the shared reading session while classmates are working on the same types of goals. Melanie's functional skill goals relating to her participation in school and classroom routines are also relatively easily entered into a matrix for the class schedule. She receives instruction and practice on her lunch, arrival, departure, and classroom

job goals at the naturally occurring times when those activities are scheduled for the entire class. At these times of day, there is a difference between Melanie's school program and that of the majority of her peers. While her peers are doing those classroom routines with general instructions and guidance from the adults in the classroom, Melanie is actually receiving instruction in her IEP goals related to completing these functional routines.

Melanie also has several social and communication goals (e.g., greeting and initiating interactions with teachers and peers, making choices, responding to yes/no questions). The benefit of using a matrix is especially evident when identifying the most appropriate times to address these embedded skill goals. To be functional for Melanie, her social-communication goals must be used within ongoing activities and routines. For example, using her communicator to greet and initiate interactions with other people is taught during times when it is natural for interactions to occur, such as during arrival, lunch, and recess. Besides indicating the most appropriate opportunities for addressing Melanie's social-communication goals, the matrix also helps to ensure that adequate opportunities for instruction in those goals are provided throughout the day. For example, Melanie's communication goal of using picture symbols and devices to answer yes/no questions is addressed not only during arrival, lunch, and break time but also during journal writing, shared reading, and math. If she did not have repeated daily opportunities to use these augmentative communication systems, Melanie would be unlikely to become proficient in their use.

Another advantage of using a matrix is that it allows the student's team to identify times for the student to receive special services, such as direct service from a speech-language therapist, physical therapist, or vision specialist. For example, Daniel, the first-grade case study student, has a goal of using his walker for 20 minutes per day. Daniel was able to practice using his walker by moving about the classroom and by traveling with the class

Program Planning Matrix

Student _Melanie_   **Class** _Ramirez/4th_   **Date** _11/2004_

Class Schedule (A.M.)

IEP GOALS	Arrival	Journal	Reading	Language skills	Break	Spelling	Math	Shared reading	Lunch
Communication									
Use pictures/devices to express needs, ask questions, initiate, make choices, answer yes/no	O	x	x	x	x	x	x	x		x
Relate recent events in two- or three-word sentences	O		x	x	x					
Functional skills									
Use picture schedule to make transitions	O	x	x	x	x	x	x	x	x	x
Arrival/departure, lunchroom routines	O	x				x				x
Follow task directions from cues	O				x		x	x		
School/classroom jobs	O	x								
Math									
Identify numbers 0–1,000	●							x		
Number line for less than, more than	●							x		
Time to minute (face, digit)	●							x		
Language arts									
Comprehension questions, novels	●			x	x					
Computer journal writing	●		x							
Read, write, spell functional vocabulary words	●				x	x				
Inventive spelling for class assignments	●		x		x	x				

Figure 4.10. Program Planning Matrix for Melanie. (Key: x = Instruction provided; O = Classroom Participation Plans with General Adaptations required; ● = General Adaptations Plan and Weekly Plan for Specific Adaptations required)

to the gym or library; however, his slow speed in using the walker made it difficult for him to keep up with his classmates. At the same time, Daniel's team had not been able to find meaningful ways for Daniel to participate in the second half of the language skills activity. Therefore, Daniel's classroom teacher would save errands for Daniel and a peer (who always completed her language skills activities quickly) to do at that time. Either the physical therapist or an instructional assistant would accompany the peer and Daniel as he used his walker for increasingly lengthy excursions around the school.

Once the IEP goals for each scheduled activity or class are identified on the Program Planning Matrix, it can be helpful to use the cells on the matrix for additional aspects of program planning. For example, the cells can be coded to indicate which type of adaptations—general and/or specific—are required for each activity. This coding is illustrated on Figure 4.10. A "○" added to a cell indicates that the general adaptations for the activity are described in a Classroom Participation Plan with General Adaptations. Where specific adaptations must be planned on a weekly or daily basis, a "•" is added to the cell. (We were not able to use color in this book, but color-coding the symbols is a better method.) Step 4 gives detailed information on the ways to actually create the plans for general and specific adaptations. Thorough descriptions of the use of the Program Planning Matrix as a tool to develop inclusive programming for students with severe disabilities are provided by Falvey (1995), Giangreco, Cloninger, and Iverson (1998), and Snell and Brown (2000).

Step 3

Strategies for Planning Adaptations: A Plan to Plan

After the team has determined when adaptations are needed, the next step is to decide how, when, and by whom the actual adaptations will be planned. The choice of adaptation planning strategies—that is, the choice of the planning methods and formats that will be used to create, record, and communicate among team members about a student's adaptations—is affected by numerous factors. These factors include the number and types of adaptations needed, the school level (i.e., elementary, middle, and high schools all present different planning challenges and advantages), teachers' schedules, the number of students with IEPs within the class, the availability of support personnel to provide in-class support, and the teachers' planning styles. The core team, especially the general and special education teachers, must decide on the ways that they will plan, communicate, and monitor the student's adaptations.

Figure 4.11, the Guide to Adaptation Planning Strategies (Individual), can be used to clarify and communicate the planning strategies agreed on by the core team. This guide is completed as soon as possible in the school year or semester and then later adjusted as necessary. It includes answers to questions such as, "When will we meet?", "How and when will we exchange materials that need to be adapted?", and "What happens if we run into problems?" A Guide to Adaptation Planning Strategies is typically most helpful when prepared for each class period at the middle school and high school levels and for the entire day at the elementary level.

The Guide to Adaptation Planning Strategies can differ according to a number of variables, including the number of students in the classroom who require individualized adaptations, the level of their support needs, and the number of adults who are involved with the classroom. With a collaborative teaming model that links particular special and general education teachers into collaborative teams that teach together across the school day, it may be more effective to create a single Guide to Adaptation Planning Strategies for the entire class rather than creating this planning guide for each student who needs individualized adaptations. The Guide to Adaptation Planning Strategies (Individual) shown in Figure 4.11 was designed specifically for Sam—a student who had more extensive and complex support needs than any of the other students with IEPs in his world geography class. However, if the team decided to develop one planning guide for the entire class, they would include information such as the following for all students with IEPs:

- Which students have adapted curricular goals?

- What planning format will be used for each student's general adaptations? When will these adaptations be developed, and by whom?

- What planning format will be used for each student's specific adaptations? When, and by whom, will these adaptations be developed?

- How and when will materials to be adapted be handled?

Guide to Adaptation Planning Strategies (Individual)

Student _____Sam_____ **Class** _World Geography/9th_ **Date** _10/2004_

Classroom Teacher _____Sailor_____ **Special Education Teacher** _____Elliott_____

Meetings: When? _Thursdays after school_ **How Long?** _15 minutes_

Planning Format: _Ms. Elliott will prepare an Adaptations Plan describing the general adaptations for each type of class activity. The Adaptations Plan will also list which activities and materials will need specific adaptations. Ms. Elliott also will prepare a form for the Weekly Plan for Specific Adaptations._

How will objectives be adapted?: ✓ Simplified ____ Altered (functional/
embedded skills)

Materials to be adapted:
✓ textbook ✓ homework ✓ worksheet ____ study guides ____ quizzes/tests
✓ other: _Ms. Elliott will prepare five daily note sheets that include the key word or concept for the day and targeted map symbols and geographic features._

Plan for exchanging materials that need to be adapted:
Tests/quizzes, study guides, and list of homework assignments that need to be adapted will be delivered at weekly planning conference. Ms. Elliot or the assistant will drop off adapted materials and tests the day before they are to be used.

Default plan: What will we do if either of us defaults on our responsibilities?
   Special education teacher: _Prepare folder of alternative activities to keep in classroom_
   Classroom teacher: _I'm on my own if I do not deliver plans/materials to be adapted to Ms. Elliot by Thursday_

Additional comments:

Figure 4.11. Guide to Adaptation Planning Strategies. (Contributed by Johnna Elliott and Cynthia Pitonyak.)

A blank form that could be used as a Guide to Adaptation Planning Strategies (Classroom) is included in Appendix A.

Step 4

Plan and Implement Adaptations: First General, Then Specific

As described in Chapter 3, dividing the adaptations process into two different levels of planning—one long term, one more short term—can help to make the process more manageable.

Step 4A: General Adaptations

Because general adaptations do not always require weekly or daily planning, they can be designed by the team and put into effect first, before plans for designing specific adaptations have been finalized. Another reason to put these adaptations in place first is that they establish the student's participation in the routines and ongoing activities of the classroom. Similar to all adaptations, they should be designed to be only as special as necessary in keeping with the hierarchy of adaptations described in Chapter 3 (see Figure 3.11).

Individualized Adaptations Plan (for Students with Simplified Curriculum Goals)

For students like Sam, whose IEP includes primarily simplified academic goals along with some functional goals in the vocational domain, a one-page Individualized Adaptations Plan (see Figure 4.12) for each class period or subject can include most of the information needed to implement the student's general adaptations, as well as notes about what specific adaptations will be planned each

week. Preliminary decisions about the class activities that would need to be adapted for Sam were made and noted on the General Assessment of Classroom Activities (see Figure 4.5, particularly the right-hand column) that was completed previously for his world geography class. Now, the general adaptations—those that apply to predictable aspects of the classroom activities and routines—are actually designed and implemented, while those that are specific are developed somewhat later.

Individualized Adaptations Plan

Student _____Sam_____ **Class** _World Geography/9th_ **Date** _10/2004_

Classroom Teacher ___Sailor___ **Special Education Teacher** ___Elliott___

Objectives: _1. Recognize and recall one main idea/concept per day_
              2. Use and define selected terms related to geographic features, map symbols

Class activity	General adaptations	Specific adaptations*
• Lecture/ discussion • Silent reading of text • Cooperative projects • Individual seatwork	• Assistant will assist Sam in using a daily note sheet to list main ideas, key concepts in his notebook. • Assistant or peer will read from the text with Sam. • Place Sam in group with peers who know him well. • Assist Sam with reading directions; provide prompts, as necessary, referring to necessary sources of information that should be used (text, notes, maps).	• Identify one main idea/concept per day. • Highlight main ideas/ key terms in text. • Identify Sam's specific tasks and contributions. • Adapt worksheets as necessary.
• Tests/ quizzes	• During class review session the day before the test, assist Sam in preparing his own study guide. Send Sam to Resource for tests; Ms. Elliott will assist with reading and recording answers, as per IEP accommodations.	• Main ideas/concepts listed on sample study guide. All tests will be adapted.
• Homework	• Prompt Sam to record assignment in his blue notebook.	• Simplify homework, reduce amount.
• Alternative activities	• If time is available because Sam has completed his work and does not have work from other classes to catch up on, he may go to the library for alternative activity (e.g., computer search related to chapter topic, current events in newspaper). Keep a record of times when alternative activities are used.	• Generate ideas for specific alternative activities related to chapter topic.

Figure 4.12. Individualized Adaptations Plan for Sam. (*Specific adaptations developed at the weekly planning meeting.) (Contributed by Johnna Elliott.)

In Sam's case, the general adaptations for his world geography class focus on the ways in which in-class assistance with note taking, silent textbook reading, and individual seat-work will be provided for him and how tests will be adapted. For example, during lecture and discussion portions of the class, the instructional assistant will assist Sam in using the daily note sheet (prepared by his special education teacher), which provides labeled spaces on which Sam is to record main ideas and key concepts. During the class review sessions on the day before each test, Sam will receive assistance in preparing a study guide. For tests, Sam will leave the classroom, and the special education teacher will read the test to Sam, an accommodation that is listed on Sam's IEP.

Although the content of the specific adaptations designed for Sam will be planned weekly, the two teachers already have determined the types of activities and materials that will require weekly planning. Each week, the teachers will identify the daily main ideas or concepts that Sam will learn, adapt any worksheets as necessary, simplify and reduce the amount of homework given to Sam, and prepare sample study guides and adapted tests.

Classroom Participation Plan with General Adaptations (for Students with Alternative Curriculum Goals)

In contrast to Sam's one-page Individualized Adaptations Plan, general adaptations for students with alternative curriculum goals will typically be more extensive and will require use of a different, more detailed planning format. Classroom Participation Plans with General Adaptations describe the ongoing adaptations to curriculum goals, instructional procedures, and/or the classroom environment that will be applied for these students. These plans, which are based on the student's IEP goals and the information gleaned from the detailed Ecological Assessment of Classroom Activities (see Figure 4.7), are usually developed by special education staff, with input from the rest of the core team. The

plans specify in respective columns 1) the classroom schedule of activities, 2) the student's goals for each activity, and 3) the general adaptations to procedures and materials that are used for instructing and supporting the student within that activity. Program plans for elementary students typically are developed for morning and afternoon sections of the daily schedule. For both middle and high school students, class-by-class planning forms typically are more useful. These planning forms are tools for communicating program plans with classroom teachers and instructional assistants and can help to maintain the integrity of instructional programming for the student.

Figure 4.13 illustrates a Classroom Participation Plan with General Adaptations for Melanie. On Melanie's Classroom Participation Plan, the class subject or activity appears in the first column. Listed in the second column are her IEP goals for each activity (as determined by using the Program Planning Matrix in Figure 4.10). The third column describes the general adaptations and procedures that should be followed to instruct or support Melanie during each activity. However, Melanie's IEP also includes some simplified goals in reading, math, and the content areas. Therefore, in the third column, the need for weekly planning of specific adaptations to these subject areas has also been noted. In addition, Melanie's plan reflects the adaptations designed to help support her behavioral needs. For example, the breaks scheduled into Melanie's day provide her with the opportunity to move around and to calm herself; these breaks are noted in the column headed "General adaptations and procedures."

Additional Options: Checklist of General Adaptations

Some teachers may prefer an adaptations plan that gives a checklist with types or categories of general adaptations that may be selected. The Checklist of General Adaptations is a form teachers can use for this

Classroom Participation Plan with General Adaptations

Student _Melanie_   **Class** _Ramirez/4th_   **Date** _9/14/2004_

Curricular Adaptations _Simplified and Alternative_

Activity	IEP goals	General adaptations and procedures
9:00–9:10 Arrival	1. Picture schedule 2. Greetings: "Hi, [name]." 3. Relate recent events in two- or three-word sentences	• Flip to picture symbol: Classroom/backpack. (**Note:** Begin each activity by having Melanie flip to appropriate symbol on picture schedule.) • Monitor putting away belongings: notebook in desk, lunchbox in cubby, backpack on hook. • Review classmates' names in photo album. Greet, socialize with peers.
9:10–9:30 Journal writing	1. Computer journal writing 2. Read, write, spell functional vocabulary words	• Melanie will tell aide or peer one thing that happened yesterday that she liked. Write it down; have her copy it on computer and then read it. (**Specific Adaptation:** Select weekly vocabulary words from Melanie's journal entry, if appropriate.)
9:30–10:15 Reading: Oral reading, discussion of text book selection	1. Comprehension questions, novels; yes/no questions 2. "Wh-" questions	• Ask Melanie yes/no questions about some aspect of the daily selection. If she answers incorrectly, restate the question. Prompt correct response after two errors. • Following oral reading of text or worksheet material, teacher will ask Melanie "wh-" questions that approximate those asked of other students (e.g., students are asked, "How did Anna relate to her new stepsister?" Melanie is asked, "Who is the sad girl in the story?") • Movement break at approximately 10:30 (**Specific adaptation:** Think of yes/no and "wh-" questions related to the daily reading selection.)
10:15–11:00 Language skills/ spelling: Individual worksheets on targeted skills	1. Inventive spelling/ class assignments 2. Follow task directions from cues 3. Read, write, spell functional words	• Select at least one vocabulary word per week from the lesson. Have Melanie make flash cards for vocabulary/spelling words. She will write or type the word (her choice) on one side of the card, cut out the picture, and paste it on the other side. Prompt her to point to and say the words. (**Specific adaptation:** Select function words; gather pictures; adapt skill worksheets as necessary; use vocabulary words in skill worksheets, if possible.)
11:00–11:30 Shared reading	1. Comprehension questions, novels 2. Expand phonemic awareness, letter–sound associations	• Alternative adaptations: Melanie will work in an individualized reading program with special ed. teacher during shared reading
11:30–12:00 Lunch	1. Follow lunch routine with minimal prompting 2. Use communication devices to initiate, make choices	• See task analysis for lunch routine • Prompt Melanie (using gestures) to point to entrée choice following cafeteria worker's cue

Figure 4.13.   Classroom Participation Plan with General Adaptations for Melanie.

purpose. (A blank version is available in Appendix A.) In the left-hand column, the class activities are listed. The third column gives a list of possible general adaptations that may be used for that activity, along with space in which to describe the nature of the adaptations to be made. In the fourth column, notes can be made about which activities will require short-term planning for specific adaptations. The Checklist of General Adaptations would serve for one subject area in an elementary classroom or for one class period at the middle-school or high-school level.

Additional Options: Behavioral Support Plans

For students with serious behavioral problems, a Behavioral Support Plan is another format for planning general adaptations. A Behavioral Support Plan includes strategies for preventing problems from occurring and instructional strategies to teach the student alternative skills to replace the problem behavior. The plan should also include responding and crisis management strategies, which may involve strategies to protect the student, as well as others, during serious incidents. More information about supporting students with serious behavior problems in inclusive environments is provided in *Behavioral Support* (Janney & Snell, 2000), another volume in the *Teachers' Guides to Inclusive Practices* series.

Step 4B: Specific Adaptations

Once general adaptations are in place, planning and implementation of specific adaptations become a priority. Specific adaptations are designed for a particular lesson or activity and require weekly or daily planning. They include simplified curriculum content and instructional adaptations designed to match a specific lesson or activity (e.g., student materials, assessments, methods for teaching a particular skill or concept).

Weekly Plans for Specific Adaptations

Weekly planning is often required for preparing specific adaptations, especially beginning in the intermediate grades and through high school as the curriculum becomes more complex and more paper-and-pencil tasks are required of students. The best possible scenario involves collaborative planning of lessons and activities by the special education and general education teachers. Not only does collaborative planning ensure that the two teachers have communicated about lesson plans and adaptations, but it also promotes greater parity in their relationship, as both teachers become more responsible for the entire classroom group. Planning forms for specific adaptations typically include 1) the daily time schedule, 2) the specific planned instructional activities, and 3) the necessary adaptations to those activities. In the beginning of the school year, the special education and general education teachers can devise a planning format suited to the schedule and sequence of activities in that class. These forms can be stored on computer files so that necessary changes in the plan can be made as the year progresses. Figure 4.14 illustrates the Weekly Plan for Specific Adaptations (Elementary) that was designed for Melanie.

Planning forms for middle or high school typically include only the adaptations designed for one particular class period. Figure 4.15 shows a planning format that is used each week to plan adaptations for Sam's ninth-grade world geography class. The first column of the table lists the typically occurring activities that need specific adaptations (based on information from the General Assessment of Classroom Activities in Figure 4.5). For Sam, these activities include in-class text reading, lectures and discussions, individual written worksheets, and tests every Friday. The second column is used to note the specific adaptations to those activities that will be required for the week. For example, during lecture and discussion portions of the class, Sam completes daily note sheets prepared by the special education teacher. These note sheets will prompt Sam to record

Weekly Plan for Specific Adaptations (Elementary)

Student _Melanie_ **Teacher/Class** _Ramírez/4th_ **Week of** _2/7/2005_ **Unit Theme** _Colonial Times_

Subjects	Class objectives	Activities	Specific adaptations
Reading/ language arts	1. Vocabulary/comprehension: _Julie and the Wolves_ 2. Written language skills: review capitalization, punctuation 3. Spelling strategies: "ie" endings	1. Use story elements and vocabulary to write new ending 2. Writer's worksheets: diary entries of boys/girls in Colonial Times 3. Skill worksheets (attached)	1. Vocabulary dictionary: Julie, wolves, trap, snow; knife, boots 2. Colonial booklet: identify key concepts and pictures; make key vocabulary into full sentences, type on computer 3. Brainstorm "ie" words after given examples; make sentences using keyboard
Science/ health	Science: animals and habitats in southwest Virginia	1. Text pp. 23–29 2. Expert groups research and present on one animal	1. Use picture prompts for text reading 2. Key concept/vocabulary: habitat, forest, wolf, cub, carnivorous 3. Group work: type draft on computer; contribute two facts
Math	Geometry: types of triangles	1. Text pp. 40–44; do problems on p. 44 2. Tangram puzzles	1. Count and write number of triangles in each category 2. Tangram puzzles with class; make tangram picture, glue down
Social skills/ class meeting	Preparation for Williamsburg field trip	1. Problem solving and role playing re: expectations, safety rules	1. Make social story including safety rules; make index cards for each site visited.

Figure 4.14.   Weekly Plan for Specific Adaptations (Elementary) for Melanie.

Weekly Plan for Specific Adaptations (Secondary)

Student _____Sam_____ **Plan for Week of** ___11/2004_____

Teacher _____Sailor_____ **Class** ___World Geography/9th____

Class activity	Specific adaptations
Lecture/discussion: *Chapters 21 & 22:* *The Middle East & North Africa* **Films:** *"The Wonder of Israel"*	Main ideas/concepts (one per day, highlighted on daily note sheets) Monday *Land mass (as compared with United States)* Tuesday *Climate: desert* Wednesday *Water as main resource* Thursday *Three major world religions developed here* Friday *Conflict: Muslim vs. Judaism*
In-class text reading	Reading for the week: *Ch. 21—highlight key concepts*
Map reading: *political, physical, population*	Maps and symbols: *names of countries, settlements near water*
Cooperative projects: *MAC Globe Project*	*Collect information for the group on population, industry versus agriculture, literacy & mortality rates. Create charts/graphs to display information.*
Individual written work	Chapter questions: *none* Worksheets: *Fill in the blanks on Venn diagram comparing and contrasting geographic elements; all students will work cooperatively, so no adaptations needed.*
Review Sessions (Thursdays) **and** **Tests** (Fridays)	*For review session on Thursday, small groups will prepare study guides; no adaptations needed; just provide occasional prompts to keep Sam on track.*
Alternative activities	*Catch up on MAC Globe project*

Figure 4.15.   Weekly Plan for Specific Adaptations (Secondary) for Sam. (Contributed by Johnna Elliott.)

information about the main ideas or concepts that have been targeted as his daily goals.

Step 5

Plan and Implement Alternative Adaptations

A student's team may decide that alternative adaptations are needed to provide types of instruction that best address a student's IEP goals. (As noted in Chapter 3, there also may be times when a team has not yet found a way to integrate a student's goals into ongoing classroom activities, and what is actually needed is better problem solving, as opposed to alternative adaptations.) For example, alternative adaptations might include the following:

- Instruction in basic or remedial reading, writing, or math

- Instruction in functional life skills and functional academics, either in school (e.g., how to use the library or the restroom) or in the community (e.g., grocery shopping or traveling in the community)

- Instruction in the development and maintenance of other individualized goals (e.g., motor, social, or communication skills)

- Vocational training and experiences

- Opportunities to preview, review, or supplement academic content

The following are brief descriptions of alternative adaptations that the teachers who contributed to this book have implemented.

Specialized Instruction in IEP Goals

Alternative adaptations activities may be needed when the process of planning a student's program reveals that the student's academic, functional, or embedded skill goals have not been addressed adequately across the day. The Program Planning Matrix (see Figure 4.10) can help to identify times when such instruction can occur without depriving the student of other important instructional opportunities. For example, Daniel was not receiving adequate amounts of time using his gait trainer (walker). Therefore, Daniel's team targeted several brief times during the day that provided logical opportunities for the physical therapist or assistant to help Daniel use his gait trainer without missing other needed instruction.

There also may be times when a student's need for developmental or remedial instruction in reading, writing, or math are such that direct instruction by a special education teacher is warranted. This is true for Melanie in the area of reading. Melanie has begun to show emergent literacy skills in her ability to point to words as a book is read aloud to her and to match words and pictures. Melanie's teacher and another fourth-grade teacher cross-group for their reading and language arts block. The 1½-hour block includes a series of small-group sessions in guided

reading, shared reading, word study, and writer's workshop. Whereas Melanie participates with a small group of classmates in guided reading and word study activities that are adapted for her, during shared reading, Melanie and two other struggling readers participate in a very structured reading lesson with the special education teacher. The lesson emphasizes phonemic awareness, basic conventions of printed language, and recognizing a few high-frequency words.

Functional Skill Instruction

According to the adaptations model, functional skill instruction is in most cases considered to be an alternative adaptation (unless instruction is in ongoing classroom routines or, for older students, is conducted as part of the general education course offerings in the school). Community-based instruction in functional skills was originally conceived as an important element of a functional, community-referenced curriculum (e.g., Brown et al., 1983). Its purpose is to teach real-life skills and activities that will enable students with severe disabilities to participate in meaningful, functional activities in their schools and communities. In inclusive elementary schools, community-based instruction is primarily conducted within the school itself, as school is the place where most elementary-age students spend their school day. That is, instruction in using the restroom, the library, the cafeteria, or in how to travel about the school would be age-appropriate, functional routines for an elementary school student. For the majority of elementary-age students with disabilities, the focus of their IEPs is on maximizing their participation in ongoing school and classroom activities.

However, in inclusive middle and high schools, some students may receive functional skill instruction outside of school. The decision to provide out-of-school learning opportunities for students with IEPs is based on the student's and family's long-term goals and on the probability that the student will require individualized, longitudinal planning and preparation for adult life in the community. After the age of 18, students with extensive support needs will spend increasing amounts of time in job settings until the end of their school programs at age 21. This change is recommended, as most students without disabilities are no longer attending high school after age 18.

Student Snapshot

Walter is in the eleventh grade. His class schedule includes basic English, geometry, health and physical education, and a 2-hour block of community-based instruction for job exploration and general community usage. Walter's IEP goals emphasize organization and self-management, functional academics, and the development of vocational skills and interests (see Figure 4.16). Four days per week, Walter works at one of a series of job training sites maintained by the high school. One day per week, he learns shopping, banking, and other skills for using consumer and community services. Walter's long-range transition plan specifies that he will have a part-time paid job in the community by the time he is 18 and completes his IEP diploma.

Alternative In-Class Activities

For various reasons, alternative activities conducted within the classroom may be considered necessary. This may occur when a class activity lasts too long for a student to participate effectively. For these occasions, lists or folders of alternative in-class activities can provide suggestions for keeping the student in the classroom and engaged in activities related to the class subject area and/or themes. For example, engaging Melanie for the entire 45-minute block designated for language arts is a challenge. Therefore, her special education teacher always keeps the classroom teacher and instructional assistant supplied with a list of alternative activities that build on any current thematic units being used

in the classroom and that emphasize written language and other goals that are appropriate for Melanie. Figure 4.17 provides an example of such a list. It includes the Multiple Intelligences Alternative Unit Activities for the Thanksgiving unit that was undertaken in Melanie's fourth-grade class. One advantage of this particular list is that it is organized according to the type of ability or intelligence— spatial, musical, body-kinesthetic, logical-mathematical, interpersonal, and intrapersonal (Gardner, 1983)—that is applied in each activity. Melanie's classroom teacher finds that this list and others like it provide her with many ideas for unit activities to do with the entire class.

Such alternative activities need to vary according to the content of class activities. The specific activities listed need to change from time to time, as the class begins new projects or themes. However, the types of activities included will generally be somewhat consistent.

These subject area or thematic lists of alternative activities may also be used during emergencies or other unforeseen circumstances. Many classroom teachers have learning centers, from which students may choose extension activities, or other ways to provide students with supplementary activities. Activities that would be appropriate for a student with an IEP can be included with these existing supplementary activity options.

Sam's world geography class provides a slightly different example of the use of alternative adaptations. Although Sam participates in virtually all of the activities that are planned for his ninth-grade world geography class, there are occasions when either he completes his work early or experiences an emotional problem that could result in a behavioral outburst. His team planned for this on his Individualized Adaptations Plan (see Figure 4.12) by noting that "if Sam has completed his work and does not have work from other classes to catch up on, he may go to the library for an alternative activity (e.g., computer search related to chapter topic, current events in newspaper)." Then, each week, on Sam's Weekly Plan for Specific Adaptations,

Program-at-a-Glance	
Student _Walter/ 11th grade_	**Date** _10/2004_

IEP goals	**IEP accommodations**
All classes • _Bring materials_ • _Take notes_ • _Participate in class discussions_ • _Complete adapted assignments and tests_ • _Follow oral directions of teacher_ • _Use self-management checks_ Math • _Practice basic operations_ • _Read and understand graphs_ • _Understand and use basic geometry terms_ • _Complete measurement of lines and angles_ English • _Locate information in reference sources_ • _Listen to literature selections and answer factual comprehension questions_ • _Compose brief journal entries and essays_ • _Keep organized notebook and assignment planner_ Transition Plan and Work Schedule • _Complete job exploration experiences_ • _Identify job interests_	• _Adapted curriculum: Basic literacy and functional applications, self-management, vocational exploration and skills_ • _Extended time on tests and projects as needed_ • _Work toward IEP diploma_
Academic/ social management needs	**Comments/special needs**
• _Walter needs prompting and positive feedback in order to maintain attention to task_ • _Monitor assignment planner notes and self-management checks_	• _Core team meeting once each marking period; whole team once per semester_

Figure 4.16. Program-at-a-Glance for Walter.

his special education teacher suggests specific alternative activities related to chapter topic (see Figure 4.15).

It is helpful to monitor the use of alternative activities. One way to do this is to include a log sheet in the student's record-keeping notebook on which the teacher or instruc-tional assistant can jot down the times when these alternative activities were used. This enables the team to do some problem solving about the times when it was difficult to in-clude the student in ongoing class activities so that the future adaptation planning can take these situations into account.

Multiple Intelligences Alternative Unit Activities

Student _____ *Melanie/ 4th grade* _____   **Date** __ *11/2004* __

Spatial (visual arts) • *Make placemats* • *Make Pilgrim hats* • *Pilgrim puzzles (clothing)* • *Make November calendar* • *Decorate bulletin board*	**Musical** • *Thanksgiving song (sing with class at start of unit activities)* • *Play musical instruments* • *Songs to go with clothing and food themes*
Body-Kinesthetic (performing movements) • *Thanksgiving finger play* • *Make sandwiches for dinner* • *Pour drinks* • *Pilgrim hat bean bag toss*	**Logical-Mathematical** (nonverbal problem solving) • *Set table: count plates, forks, cups, and so on* • *Make cornucopia centerpiece with picture cues and numbers (e.g., five apples, two squash)*
Intrapersonal (personal meaning) • *Family picture book* • *Invite parents to "dinner"* • *All decorations go home to be part of family Thanksgiving celebration*	**Interpersonal** (communication/interaction) • *Match and write words with family pictures* • *Thanksgiving symbol board* • *Make "dinner" for peers and family*

Figure 4.17. Multiple Intelligences Alternative Unit Activities for Melanie. (Contributed by Cynthia Pitonyak.)

Step 6

Monitor and Evaluate

This section briefly addresses some key issues related to how the core and extended teams will communicate about and evaluate adaptations and support plans. *Collaborative Teaming* (Snell & Janney, 2005), another volume in the *Teachers' Guides to Inclusive Practices* series, goes into greater depth about these processes and also discusses ways to communicate about adaptation plans in classrooms in which several students with disabilities are supported by a team of general and special educators.

Team Planning and Problem-Solving Meetings

Designing adaptations, like teaching in general, requires ongoing evaluation and problem solving. Each teaching team needs to be familiar with some processes and strategies that they can use when new adaptations are needed or when existing adaptations need evaluation and possibly revision.

Adaptations planning for some students (e.g., Vanessa, who has a learning disability) may not require separate meetings of the student's core IEP team. In other cases (e.g., Walter, who has mental retardation but only limited support needs), planning and problem-solving meetings may occur once each semester or grading period. In a few cases, such as for core teams that serve students with extensive learning and support needs more similar to Daniel's or Melanie's, a monthly planning and problem-solving meeting may be required. These regularly scheduled monthly meetings serve to review progress, revise long-term general adaptations as necessary, conduct some creative problem solving regarding specific adaptations, and make plans to address any other issues or concerns team members might have. In addition, a mechanism for planning short-term specific adaptations may be required for students with altered curriculum goals and extensive support needs. These meetings typically involve a subset of the members of the student's core team—sometimes just the general and special education teachers—and may be held weekly or biweekly.

It is to everyone's advantage to make these meetings as efficient as possible. Some strategies to promote efficiency include assigning specific roles (facilitator, recorder, timekeeper, and so on), having a written agenda, and keeping strict time limits. Figure 4.18 shows an example of a simple Team Meeting Agenda and Minutes form used at monthly core team meetings for Melanie. The team works from a written agenda and strictly adheres to its 30-minute time schedule. Melanie's IEP service coordinator takes responsibility for taking minutes at team meetings and making copies of the minutes to distribute to each team member. Some school teams have had the form printed on pressure-sensitive carbon paper so that at the end of the meeting, each person can keep a copy. This helps to ensure that team members know exactly what actions they have agreed to implement.

Team Meeting Agenda and Minutes

Student _Melanie_   **Teacher/Grade** _Ramirez/4th_   **Date** _10/4/2004_

People Present _Johnson (fourth-grade teacher), Pitonyak (IEP manager), Larsen_
(instructional assistant), Miotta (physical therapist)

Agenda Items/Decisions

1. *Classroom observations: Pitonyak to complete art and math this week.*
2. *Food allergies: For now, cannot have ANY food not sent from home. Inform Melanie's mom of any slip-ups. She's going to a nutritional specialist next week and will give us more information.*
3. *Communication: Pitonyak to complete communication demand log this week; will be kept in a notebook.*
4. *Peer interactions: Larsen to take peer photos for communication book this week.*

Next Meeting

Date: _11/8_   **Time:** _8:00 a.m._ **Who:** _Full Team_

Agenda Items:

1. *Where to brush teeth*
2. *Schedule messy activities that require handwashing?*
3. *Times for therapists to be in classroom*

Figure 4.18.   Team Meeting Agenda and Minutes for Melanie's IEP team. (Contributed by Cynthia Pitonyak.)

Monitoring and Evaluating Individualized Adaptations

The way in which staff members monitor programs and keep records about students' learning progress also changes when students with IEPs are included in general classrooms. A number of teachers and assistants may instruct and support the student and, thus, may need access to information about the student's program. It is important to guard the confidentiality of students' medical records and specific diagnoses while still keeping instructionally relevant information accessible to teachers and assistants.

Student Record Keeping

Large three-ring binders are handy to use as planning and monitoring notebooks for students who require extensive adaptations. Special education teachers who serve several or all of the students with IEPs in a given classroom may find it easiest to keep one notebook per classroom. Those who serve students across several classrooms may find individual student notebooks more helpful. The notebook provides a convenient vehicle for communication among team members. For each student, include the following information, as relevant:

- Student Information Form (p. 127)
- Program-at-a-Glance (p. 128)
- Daily/weekly classroom schedule
- Related services schedule
- General Assessment of Classroom Activities (p. 129)
- Ecological Assessment of Classroom Activities (p. 130)
- Program Planning Matrix (p. 131)
- Guide to Adaptation Planning Strategies (Individual) (p. 132)
- Individualized Adaptations Plan (p. 134) or Classroom Participation Plan with General Adaptations (p. 135)

- Weekly Plan for Specific Adaptations (pp. 136 or 137)
- Lists of supplementary activities
- Log of times when alternative adaptations were used
- Tests and other written materials to be adapted
- Team Meeting Agenda and Minutes (p. 139)
- Team Evaluation of Student Adaptations (p. 140)
- Data sheets and anecdotal records for monitoring IEP objectives
- Home communication log
- Student work samples

Evaluating Student Adaptations

It is important for teams to periodically evaluate their functioning as a team and the quality of the work they are accomplishing. The most effective teams stop to ask one another, "How are we doing?" Student support teams also need to ask whether the adaptations they have developed are helping students to participate actively in the classroom and to meet their learning goals while still being only as special as necessary. Some sample questions that team members may want to ask themselves are provided in the Team Evaluation of Student Adaptations (available on p. 140 of Appendix A). Completing and discussing such an evaluation helps team members to ensure that the student is receiving high-quality inclusive programming and that the team members feel focused and effective working together.

PUTTING THE STEPS TOGETHER

To provide an example of how the adaptation planning process looks when it is used to plan for an individual student, the steps that Daniel's core team took to plan for his year in first grade are described in the following paragraphs. It is important to note that Daniel is a student with significant multiple disabilities whose programming requires the planning steps and tools marked with brackets on Figure 4.1. Daniel's need for a significantly altered curriculum goals and physical support require this level of planning. In contrast, students with less extensive support needs typically do not require weekly planning time set aside specifically for them alone.

In June, during the week before school ended, Cyndi Pitonyak, the special education consulting teacher, shared Daniel's Student Information Form (see Figure 4.3) and Program-at-a-Glance (see Figure 4.4) with Renata James, the first-grade teacher. Because Ms. Pitonyak had previously supported other students in Ms. James's classroom and was familiar with the classroom routines, she and Ms. James already had completed the General Assessment of Classroom Activities (see Figure 4.5). When school started in late August, Ms. Pitonyak conducted observation sessions across several days to complete Ecological Assessments of Classroom Activities (see Figure 4.7, which assesses Daniel's current level of participation and the need for supports and adaptations). During this time, Ms. Pitonyak also drafted Daniel's Program Planning Matrix (see Figure 4.10), tentatively identifying the classroom activities during which each of Daniel's IEP goals would be addressed.

During the second week of school, Daniel's core team, including Ms. Pitonyak, Ms. James, Daniel's parents, the instructional assistant, and the physical therapist, met to brainstorm about adaptations for Daniel. The team discussed each classroom routine and activity to generate creative and educationally relevant ways to enhance Daniel's participation in the classroom. At the end of this meeting, Ms. Pitonyak and Ms. James completed the Guide to Adaptation Planning Strategies (see Figure 4.11). They tentatively agreed to meet for 20 minutes each Thursday, while the students were participating in music class, to plan for the following week. Because Ms. Pitonyak also provided consultative services for three other students in Ms. James's class, the two teachers

would also use this planning time to collaboratively design activities to accommodate both Daniel and the other students with IEPs and to generate ideas for specific adaptations. In addition, grade-level planning with the first-grade team incorporated consideration of Daniel's and the other students' individualized curriculum goals and IEP accommodations.

Throughout September, Ms. Pitonyak observed Daniel in the classroom and drafted Classroom Participation Plans with General Adaptations (see Figure 4.13) for Daniel's participation in predictable class routines and activities. She reviewed these draft plans with Ms. James and the instructional assistant and modeled some of the teaching techniques that seemed to work best for Daniel. Until these Classroom Participation Plans were firmly in place, Ms. Pitonyak and Ms. James did not hold their weekly meeting to plan specific adaptations. Instead, Ms. Pitonyak checked in daily with Ms. James while the students were in art, music, or physical education class to learn about specific materials and activities that were planned for the following day.

The main activities that required specific adaptations for Daniel were math and language arts. When Ms. Pitonyak and Ms. James began holding weekly planning meetings during the last week of September, they discussed the specific adaptations needed for the following week. They also discussed any problems that had arisen and made any necessary adjustments to Daniel's instructional program plans and general adaptations.

Also during September, a team meeting that included the physical, occupational, and speech-language therapists was held. At this meeting, the team discussed ways to integrate Daniel's communication and motor skill needs into his classroom activities. The group scheduled in-class sessions with the vision teacher twice per week during language skills activities. Pull-in physical therapy was scheduled during physical education class, which provided a natural opportunity to overlap some of Daniel's motor goals with those of his classmates. Occupational therapy sessions were scheduled twice per week during learning centers, during which Daniel could use his walker to move from one center to another and could handle the manipulative materials that were used for center activities. After seeing the Multiple Intelligences Alternative Activities List that Ms. Pitonyak had developed for the Thanksgiving unit (see Figure 4.17), the four teachers on the first-grade team decided to generate a supplementary activity list to coordinate with each thematic unit completed by their grade level. These alternative activities would extend the unit into the tactile and kinesthetic modes that were so important for Daniel because of his visual impairment. Ms. Pitonyak and the instructional assistant kept a record in Ms. James's class notebook of the times when these alternative activities were used because specific adaptations had not been designed in advance for Daniel.

Daniel's full team, including his parents, Ms. James, Ms. Pitonyak, the vision teacher, the occupational therapist, the physical therapist, and the instructional assistant, scheduled a meeting once every 6 weeks. At these meetings, the team reviewed Daniel's progress and evaluated the adaptations they had been using by completing and discussing the Team Evaluation of Student Adaptations. They did further brainstorming about difficulties and made plans for the next 6 weeks, recording their decisions on the Team Meeting Agenda and Minutes (see Figure 4.18).

Chapter 5

Adapting Instructional Activities
in Basic Skills and Content Areas

This chapter provides examples of ways to design and adapt instructional activities so that heterogeneous groups of students can participate in shared learning experiences. Although the adaptations designed for each student must be individualized, it is helpful to see or read about some of the adaptations that other teachers have devised for their students. Therefore, several lists of possible adaptations for some of the basic skills (reading, writing, and math) and the content areas (science and social studies) instructional activities encountered in inclusive classrooms are also provided.

TWO REMINDERS: START WITH ACCOMMODATING TEACHING AND THE STUDENT'S GOALS IN MIND

General education classroom teachers, who are used to planning instruction for groups of students who participate in the standard grade-level curriculum, may be nervous about the idea of teaching students for whom this curriculum is not completely suitable. Including students with disabilities in general education classes requires rethinking the idea that all students in a class must learn the same things at the same time. Instead, what is important is that classmates share a community and a common context for their learning experiences. Students can benefit, both academically and socially, from working together in shared activities, even if the objectives they accomplish within those activities are varied.

The adaptation strategies offered in this chapter maintain the assumption that accommodating teaching practices are, in a sense, a prerequisite to making individualized adaptations. The strategies described under each curriculum area (reading, writing, math, and the content areas) follow the hierarchy of least-to-most intrusive adaptations that was presented in Chapter 3 (see Figure 3.11). That is, we first say a few words about accommodating teaching practices in each cur-

riculum area, describe some curricular and instructional adaptations for typical instructional activities, and then give suggestions for alternative adaptations.

In our adaptations model (presented in Chapter 3), we describe three types of curricular adaptations: supplementary, simplified, and alternative. This chapter focuses on the adaptations needed for students with simplified and alternative curricular goals, rather than those whose primary curricular modification is the addition of supplementary goals in organization, study skills, learning strategies, or social and behavioral skills that may indeed be very important and effective in aiding some students' achievement. These students (who often are classified as having learning disabilities or emotional/behavioral disorders) typically participate in the general curriculum but receive accommodations to teaching and testing, which should be provided during ongoing classroom instruction (see Figure 5.1).

Recall that when a student's individual curriculum goals for a particular subject area or activity differ in scope or complexity from those of classmates, these are *simplified* curriculum goals. Other students may have *altered* curriculum goals drawn from the functional or embedded skill areas. Within a given instructional activity, most of the students in the class may be working on goals that are drawn from the general education curriculum for their grade level, some students may be working on simplified goals from that same subject area, and a smaller number of students may be working on goals that are drawn from different subject or skill areas. When a student has adaptations that do not enable participation in the same instructional activity as classmates, those are alternative adaptations. (Others who have written about curricular adaptations have used the term *multilevel curriculum* to refer to lessons in which objectives with varying degrees of difficulty have been identified for various students. *Curriculum overlap* refers to lessons for which students' objectives are drawn from different subject or skill areas [Collicott, 1991; Giangreco & Putnam, 1991].)

	English	Math	Social studies
Unit goal for all students	*Will collect, organize, and share information about a concept through reading, listening, verbalizing and writing*	*Will use various computations and measurements to solve problems*	
Lesson objective for most students	*To read and verbally tell stories*	*To determine and use the appropriate type of computations to solve problems*	*To define and spell unit vocabulary and use it appropriately in written and oral activities*
Simplified lesson objective for one student	*To listen to stories and retell them*	*Given a choice of + or −, to select and use the appropriate type of computation to solve problems*	*To read, write, spell, and define key unit vocabulary (approximately five concepts per unit)*
Altered/ functional lesson objective for one student	*To introduce the story presentations using a prerecorded message on an augmentative communication device*	*To use predetermined amount strategy (money envelopes) to purchase items for the group's observation and study*	*To identify animals and common objects associated with unit themes by pointing to pictures*

Figure 5.1.   Adapted curriculum objectives that maintain access to the general curriculum.

For example, in Chapter 3, we examine the ways in which adaptations were planned for Melanie, the fourth-grader whose IEP includes both simplified and altered curriculum goals. The approaches used by Melanie's fourth-grade teacher illustrate the ways that Melanie's goals can, for the most part, be met without using alternative adaptations. Thus, during the majority of reading, writing, and math activities, Melanie worked on simplified versions of the class activity. For example, during writer's workshop sessions, Melanie participated along with her classmates. She was completing sentence starters or story frames, however, whereas other students were generating their own topics and organizing their ideas. At other times of day, the focus of her instruction was on functional routines and embedded skills, such as using a picture schedule, completing the arrival routine, or using her communication systems to make

choices. Thus, in social studies, Melanie worked with a cooperative group to make a model to illustrate their project on the shrinking habitat for black bears. Whereas the focus for classmates was on the social studies content that was used in making the model, the focus of Melanie's participation was on the motor and communication skills involved in constructing the model, with a secondary focus on reading, writing, and spelling key unit vocabulary terms.

Therefore, the special and general education teaching team must plan for all students from the start. Be sure that general education teachers, special education teachers, and paraprofessionals are familiar with students' IEP goals in the areas of reading and writing and have copies of their Programs-at-Glance.

Each of the following sections first addresses some accommodating teaching practices for the subject area under consideration, then provides suggestions for making curricular and instructional adaptations, and finally describes some alternative adaptations in that subject area.

READING AND WRITING

The starting point is accommodating literacy instruction—that is, the use of methods and materials that will reach most learners most of the time. Next, individualized adaptations are made for students who have special needs in the area of literacy, beginning with the least intrusive or least special adaptations.

Accommodating Reading and Writing Instruction

Regardless of the debates about best approaches to teaching literacy, it is clear that students learn to read and write by devoting significant time to reading, listening, speaking, and writing. A classroom that provides a rich array of types and levels of print materials, technology for accessing print in alternative ways, and a large proportion of time dedicated to literacy instruction lays the foundation for success. A well-balanced literacy program addresses skills for word study or word attack (e.g., phonological awareness, letter identification, sound–symbol relationships, decoding word patterns), fluency, and comprehension through authentic activities that involve reading and writing for information and pleasure.

In the primary classroom, organizing literacy instruction into what Cunningham, Hall, and Sigmon (1999) called "the four blocks" is a way to ensure that all students, including both eager and struggling readers, are accommodated within the program. The four blocks—Guided Reading, Self-Selected Reading, Writing, and Working with Words—use a combination of large and small groups, partner and independent activities, and teacher-selected and student-selected reading

materials. This combination of a variety of groupings and both self-selected and teacher-selected materials enables students with special needs to participate in some activities with curricular and/or instructional adaptations and, if necessary, to receive alternative adaptations for others.

For example, the teacher might introduce a new piece of informational text to the class as a large group, completing a KWL (What We **K**now—What We **W**ant to Find Out—What We **L**earned) chart or doing other activities to activate prior knowledge, create motivation, and establish a shared context among the students. Certain vocabulary might be introduced to the class as a whole, especially if the reading relates to a thematic unit. Next, students might read the text in small, teacher-supported groups or with partners. (Some students might even read independently.) These groups would work on a range of customized word identification, fluency, and/or comprehension strategies, depending on the needs of the group members. The third activity might involve writing a response to the reading in a literature journal. (See the section on literature journals.) Finally, students could be involved in a variety of either support or extension activities, in which alternative adaptations are provided for struggling readers.

Curricular and Instructional Adaptations for Reading and Writing

Supporting struggling readers and students whose oral and/or written communication involves the use of assistive technology and even other symbol systems within activities that place significant reading and writing demands on students can be a challenge (see Figure 5.2). This section provides an array of suggestions for adapting some of the reading and written language activities encountered in elementary and middle school: word study; comprehension; literature study, book circles, or novel groups; spelling; and writing assignments.

Numerous assistive technology devices, as well as hardware and software adaptations to make computer technology accessible, can enable students with cognitive, physical, or sensory disabilities to participate in their classroom community and access the general curriculum. Assistive technology includes devices and adaptations for:

- Computer access
- Mobility
- Augmentative and alternative communication
- Low-tech adaptations including Velcro, laptrays, and writing utensils

Decisions related to the selection of assistive technology should address:

- What is needed to enable the student to accomplish the specific activity as independently as possible
- The student's particular abilities, needs, and limitations
- Aesthetics and age-appropriateness
- Portability and ease of use
- Reliability

For more information on assessing and selecting students' assistive technology needs, see the resource list in Appendix B.

Figure 5.2. Assistive technology for inclusive classrooms.

Adapting Word Study (Word Recognition/Vocabulary)

- Use easier words or fewer words.

- Use words from the student's experience and words that are used in multiple contexts across the day.

- Use semantic mapping to create visual representations of how words are related conceptually.

- Provide magnetic letter boards for practicing new sounds and letters.

- Provide dry-erase boards for practicing new sounds, letters, or words.

- Have the student match words and pictures, rather than saying or writing them.

Adapting Comprehension

- Use prediction strategies to activate prior knowledge and give a purpose for reading. Before reading or listening to a story, have students read the title and chapter titles and look at the pictures. Ask questions such as, "What does the title make you think about?" "Where do you think the story takes place?" "What do you think will happen in the story?"

- Use the KWL strategy when introducing and reviewing informational texts.

- Teach students to use metacognitive strategies to ask themselves, "What is my purpose for reading this selection?"

- Teach summarizing and paraphrasing.

- Use reciprocal teaching: Teach students to do summarizing, questioning, and predicting (Palincsar & Brown, 1984).

- Provide text enhancements, including illustrations, diagrams, and concept maps.

- Make story maps or other graphic organizers with labeled spaces where students can write the setting, characters, problem, and solution.

- Teach questioning strategies such as the "Here, Hidden, Head" strategy. The answers to literal or factual comprehension questions are "here" on the page—the reader can point to them. The answers to inferential questions are "hidden"—clues or hints are provided in the book, but the reader has to draw conclusions using the clues provided. The answers to evaluative questions are in one's own "head"—they are subjective, not based on objective facts.

- For a student who does not read, have the student sequence pictures of the main events from the story.

- Adapt the format of the text: Enlarge the text, rewrite it at lower readability, tape record the text, or scan texts into talking computer programs.

- Allow a student to give oral rather than written responses to reading comprehension questions.

- Ask a student only factual questions, such as who, what, where, and when questions.

- Allow a student to draw pictures to illustrate a story, rather than writing or answering oral questions.

- Have a student sequence pictures of events in the story, rather than writing or answering oral questions.

- Provide predictable, repetitive books. (This also enhances fluency.)

- Use repeated readings. (This also enhances fluency.)

Adapting Spelling

- Use fewer words.

- Use words from reading, writing, or content area activities.

- Have the student use an electronic communicator rather than spelling words orally.

- Teach the strategy: Say the word, spell it, write it, cover it, write it, and compare.

- Ask the student to match pictures with words, instead of spelling the words.

- Read the words for a spelling test and have the student write the first letter only.

- Provide an adapted test for the student that lists two or more spelling words beside each number. Have the student circle the word as he or she hears it read.

- Ask the student to circle the picture from an array of two or three pictures as he or she hears each word during a spelling test.

Adapting Literature Study, Book Circles, or Novel Units

A literature study, book circle, or novel unit approach typically includes a variety of listening, oral or silent reading, writing, and comprehension activities. Students are often given opportunities to choose the reading material and the methods they will use to study the novel. An array of suggestions for adapting literature study or novel unit activities follows. Depending on the student's curricular adaptations, these strategies either simplify the reading task (e.g., by providing text enhancements or simplified reading material) or bypass oral reading and word identification and focus on other skills and concepts that can be developed through the novel unit activities. (Many of these ideas were contributed by Kenna Colley.)

- Select novels of varying degrees of difficulty, all with the same theme. Assign students to groups based on their reading level, or give all students a choice between two or three books. (Appendix B includes a list of publishers of high interest/low readability fiction and nonfiction, including adapted and illustrated classics.)

- Listen to a book on audiotape, or watch a movie in addition to, or instead of, reading the book.

- Preview and preread the book with a peer tutor, special educator, or volunteer.

- Bypass word identification, and focus just on comprehension: Read the novel aloud to the student either one-to-one or in a small group. Frequently pose comprehension questions during reading.

- Use story maps: The student, peers, or an adult can draw story strips or pictures as the story progresses. These materials can then serve as picture cues (text enhancements) for discussing story grammar and the sequence and meaning of events in the story. Or the story map can be an adaptation of the personal written response assignment given to most students in the class.

- Create a picture dictionary of characters and important objects from the story (e.g., for *Julie of the Wolves*, include Julie, wolves, snow, knife, boots, and trap). The student can refer to the dictionary when answering questions or writing about the novel. Or creating the dictionary and labeling the pictures can be the student's response task.

- Make a story grammar booklet or a comprehension booklet with pictures. The pictures can be photocopies from the original book; drawn by adults, peers, or the student; cut from magazines; or printed from a graphics computer program. The booklet should include text that summarizes the story at an appropriate readability level for the student.

- Create story grammar envelopes (i.e., an envelope each for characters, setting, problem, and solution). Ask story grammar questions and then write the answers on cards. The student puts these in the appropriate envelopes and then uses the envelopes to create story webs, write chapter summaries, or review for tests.

- Make puppets of the main characters and present a play based on the story.

- Sort pictures of characters and objects of the story according to various attributes. For example, the animals might go on one page and the people on another page.

- Make a poster or brochure about the book.

- When written responses are required, provide writing frames. The student is given a structured page that focuses on general story grammar or on one element of story grammar (see Figure 5.3).

Adapting Writing Assignments (including literature journals, personal journals, or self-selected writing projects)

- Provide stimulus questions. For literature journals, post a list of daily journal stimulus questions for the whole class or put a list of questions inside the front cover of individual students' journals. For the student who cannot be successful with a blank page, structure the student's daily entry by writing the specific questions he or she is to answer that day. These questions can be selected in collaboration with the student in a brief interview. Here are a few examples of stimulus questions and adapted questions written at a lower readability level:

  1. *Stimulus question:* Which character did you empathize with most? Why?

     Adapted question: What person in the story did you like the best?

  2. *Stimulus question:* What was the most significant aspect of the story you read today? Reflect on why you selected that aspect.

     Adapted question: What was the best part of the story you read today?

  3. *Stimulus question:* What emotions did you experience while reading today? Reflect on the specific elements of the story that evoked those emotions.

     Adapted question: How did you feel while reading today? Sad? Happy?

- Provide sentence starters or use a cloze procedure rather than requiring the student to write complete sentences. For example, if students have read *Charlotte's Web* and most students are to respond to the question "How does Wilbur feel about Charlotte at first?" the student might be given the following cloze sentence: "Wilbur thought Charlotte was _____ and _____." If necessary, provide a word bank from which the student can select and copy the answers. Or, for the student who does not write, provide printed adhesive labels that the student can peel off and stick in the blank.

Literature Journal Frame

Date: _____   Last page number: _____   Book: _____

_____

Author: _____

Why did you pick this book? _____

_____

Who is in this story so far? _____

What is the main thing that happened in the story today? _____

_____

Story Grammar Frame

Book: _____

Chapter: _____

Main characters: _____

Where? _____

What happened? _____

_____

Personal Journal Frame

Name: _____   Date: _____

Today, we have   Art   Music   P.E.   Library

The weather today is: _____

My classroom job for the day is: _____

_____

Figure 5.3.   Writing frames. (Contributed by Christine Burton.)

- Provide a scribe. (Pair a student who has difficulty with independent writing with another student who is a more competent writer or with an adult). After the scribe writes what the student has said, the student may copy it on paper, copy it on the computer, draw pictures, or cut-and-paste illustrations.

- Provide writing frames. Students who need support with basic comprehension and writing can be given a structured page that provides questions and spaces for answers, with some students expected to write complete sentences and others expected to write a word or two. A student also could be provided with a word bank to use in filling in the blanks. For example, after a daily novel reading session, the writing frame might provide space for the student to name the main character, setting, and what happened. A teacher, assistant, or peer writes the responses on a card, and the student copies the information onto the frame under the correct heading. Alternatively, the student might be given one or more sentence starters or a writing frame, such as those illustrated in Figure 5.3.

• Students who are not able to participate in writing activities can create products such as posters, dioramas, mobiles, and paintings. The student presents the final product to the class using his or her own words or other communicative methods.

Alternative Adaptations for Reading and Writing

If students participate in separate literacy instruction, these alternative adaptations should indeed be specialized: The instruction should utilize effective, evidence-based practices; be very focused and prescriptive; and be coordinated with literacy activities in the classroom. As Cunningham and Allington noted,

> Struggling readers who participate in remedial or resource room instructional support programs are the very children who need the kind of reading instruction that is coherently planned and richly integrated. . . . Special programs are most effective when they provide supportive instruction that is designed to ease the difficulties that participating children are having in their classrooms. (2003, p. 204)

It is preferable to think of alternative literacy instruction as supplementary to the instruction occurring in the regular class, rather than as a replacement for it. Alternative literacy instruction may be remedial—that is, designed to remedy the student's weak literacy skills and help the student to progress as far as possible within the typical scope of literacy skills. Or the alternative instruction may be compensatory, if the purpose is to provide the student with functional reading and writing skills or, at an even more basic level, to teach the student to manage and respond to symbol systems that are encountered within daily life. Sample lesson sequences—one for a remedial program and one for a student needing a compensatory or functional approach—are offered in Figure 5.4.

Ad Hoc Groupings of Students with and without Disabilities for Review or Corrective Lessons

Another way to provide alternative adaptations in reading or writing is to use ad hoc

---

Remedial or Developmental Lesson

1. Read one or two known books.
2. Read yesterday's new book, take a running record.
3. Learn through a skill lesson, based on miscues and/or letter–sound practice.
4. Do a language experience activity.
5. Rearrange a cut-up story.
6. Read a new book.

Functional Reading Lesson

1. Present organizing questions: who, what, when, where.
2. Dictate a language experience story.
3. Point-read a story together with a peer.
4. Choose and list vocabulary words (not more than four new words at a time.)
5. Put words on index cards.
6. Say, spell, trace, and spell.
7. Reread a story.
8. Read sight words on index cards (at least 80% known words).

Figure 5.4. Sample lesson sequences for alternative reading instruction. (Contributed by Christine Burton.)

groupings of students for review or corrective lessons. Ad hoc groupings avoid identifying particular students as being always in need of extraordinary assistance. Instead of identifying permanent remedial groups, students can be identified for review or corrective sessions based on their need for specific prerequisite skills required to participate in class instruction. For example, one special education consulting teacher developed a writing laboratory as an alternative activity for a second-grade class that included Joel, a student with mental retardation. Three times per week, Joel and a small group of classmates went to the consulting teachers' office for a writing laboratory, while other students in the class were engaged in their writer's workshop activities. The students who participated in the writing laboratory with Joel were selected by the general education teacher based on her evaluations of the previous week's writer's workshop activities. In the writing laboratory, the special education teacher provided Joel and his classmates with small-group and individualized instruction that focused on the specific written language skills with which they were having difficulty.

Lists or Folders of Alternative Activities

When the class activity lasts too long for a student to maintain focus, when a planned adaptation has failed, or perhaps when the student needs a break from the usual schedule, lists or folders of alternative in-class activities can provide suggestions for keeping the student in the classroom and engaged in activities related to the class subject area and/or themes. For example, engaging a student during a lengthy block designated for a writer's workshop can be a challenge. Lists or folders of alternative activities can be used as cushion activities, both for students who need alternative adaptations and also other students in the class who may complete tasks ahead of time and need cushion activities. Figure 5.5 provides a Writer's Workshop Supplementary Activity List.

MATH

The difficulties that students may have with math range from poor organizational skills that interfere with the execution of paper-and-pencil operations to cognitive disabilities that hinder abstract thinking and, therefore, the comprehension of certain mathematical concepts.

Accommodating Instruction in Math

Carnine (1998) gave these components of effective mathematics instruction for students with learning disabilities:

1. Focus on big ideas (i.e., generalizable concepts)

2. Establish motivation and relevance by working real problems and conducting investigations

3. Use direct instruction following the instructional sequence of a) demonstration, b) guided practice, and c) independent practice

In addition, mathematics instruction that accommodates the learning characteristics of students with many disabilities, as well as many students without disabilities, begins with the use of concrete models and demonstrations, then progresses to the use of pictorial or graphic representations, and finally moves to the abstract level and the use of symbols. (For example, when teaching about money, begin with real coins and bills, then use pictures of money, and finally move to the use of numerals and dollar signs.)

Curricular and Instructional Adaptations in Math

As is true for other subject areas, the decision about how to adapt a particular mathematics lesson is determined by the student's goals.

Writer's Workshop Supplementary Activity List

____ Choose a category: animals, foods, or people. Write a member of the category for each letter of the alphabet.

____ Draw an outline of an object. Brainstorm all of the words you know that describe the object and write them inside the outline.

____ Cut a food picture from a magazine and write 10 words that describe the food.

____ Make lists of sights, sounds, and smells.

____ If all the words in the world except five were taken away, which five would you keep? Why?

____ Write telegrams with only 15 words allowed.

____ List color words and describe how they look, taste, feel, or smell (e.g., green is sour, pink is sweet).

____ Cut words from a magazine to make a mystery message.

____ Go outside with chalk and write a note on the sidewalk.

____ Write horoscopes for classmates, teachers, and family members.

____ Taste a food or drink, then write an advertisement about it.

____ Read the beginning of a book or story and write your own ending.

____ Write recipes for some of your favorite foods.

____ Write clues about an object and have others try to guess what it is.

____ Write a list of "Don't you just hate it when . . .".

____ Write about your dreams.

____ Write invitations to go on exciting trips, such as a safari, river rafting trip, or whale watch.

____ Write "Yellow Pages" for your school. Include all of the services that are available and make advertisements for them.

____ Interview people around the school. Describe each person's life, likes, dislikes, and important things he or she wants to accomplish.

____ Write a postcard from a faraway place to a friend or family member.

____ Cut out a comic strip. Write new dialogue for it.

____ Write about "The Camping Trip I'll Never Forget."

____ Use a calendar and make up a saying for each of the 12 months. Try to make your saying match the picture on the calendar.

____ Write a poem using all of the names of the days of the week.

____ Write a story about an airplane ride, and then make the paper into an airplane to fly.

____ Fold a piece of your writing into a present, tie it with ribbon or string, and give it to your teacher to open.

____ Make a touch-and-tell scrapbook. Collect samples of things that are interesting to touch and write descriptive words next to each.

____ Make a "wanted" poster about your teacher or one of your classmates.

____ Bring a photo album from home, or use a communication book. Type the names of selected pictures.

____ Describe a special program, film, or book that your class has seen or read recently.

____ List several of the items from the day's lunch menu. Say and type them.

Figure 5.5. Writer's Workshop Supplementary Activity List. (Contributed by Kenna Colley.)

The math section of some students' IEPs essentially comprises accommodations (e.g., untimed tests, test directions read aloud) and possibly some supplementary goals in learning strategies or organizational skills. Simplified curricular goals in math are appropriate for some students who are able to learn mathematical concepts and processes but not at the same rate or level of difficulty as their classmates. These students may have simplified math goals on their IEPs, as well as accommodations such as more time, the use of manipulatives, and access to calculators. Students whose IEPs include alternative goals in math include those who are learning basic number concepts and computations, time, and money for the functional use of numbers in daily life. Other students' altered math goals essentially bypass the use of number concepts and instead emphasize adapted routines and the use of symbol systems to enable participation in daily activities involving money and time (Ford et al. 1989; Snell & Brown, 2000).

The following is an array of some possible ways to adapt math instruction:

- Allow the student to continue to use manipulatives and/or pictorial representations of number concepts and processes after classmates have moved to abstract representations.

- Teach mnemonics (e.g., **P**lease **E**xcuse **M**y **D**ear **A**unt **S**ally for the order of algebraic operations [parentheses, exponents, multiply, divide, add, subtract]), and prompt the student to use them at appropriate times.

- Provide posters (on the walls and/or in smaller versions at students' desks) that cue students to the operations used in word problems (e.g., "Words that mean addition: plus, more, more than, add, increase").

- Add cues to computation problems in texts and worksheets, such as " + means add" and "– means subtract." Or use highlighters to color code computational signs: green for addition and red for subtraction.

- Allow the use of a calculator, number line, or multiplication table.

- Box computation items for students.

- Reduce the amount or complexity of problems done by the student. For example, have the student complete only the two-digit multiplication problems on a page of two- and three-digit problems.

- Allow students to use graph paper or turn lined paper sideways so that the lines become vertical columns.

- Fold worksheets so students can work on one row at a time.

- Highlight directions and cues.

- On worksheets, reduce the number of items per page.

- Have the student complete fewer items (e.g., only every other item).

- Use large-print materials or make photocopied enlargements.

- Provide an example on worksheets and tests.

- Provide answer boxes.

- Provide self-instructional training: Teach students to say the steps to themselves as they work a computation.

- Provide more cues, prompts, and feedback as a student completes practice activities.

- Change the task requirements for text or worksheet exercises. For example, have the student circle numerals named by the teacher rather than computing the problems on a math assignment. Or rewrite the directions: "Circle each 7."

- Provide choices for the answers to text or worksheet exercises. For example, on a worksheet with clock faces and blank lines on which students are to write the time, write in two choices and have the student circle the correct time.

Alternative Adaptations for Math

As is the case for reading and writing, alternative adaptations for math may be either remedial or compensatory. That is, students may be participating in instruction that is designed to correct and accelerate their math skills, or they may be learning to use numbers in functional applications for everyday life. Functional math focuses on basic numeracy skills, time management, and money skills that will enable the person to participate as actively as possible in life at home, school, work, and in the community.

One strategy to allow remedial work in math without using a pull-out approach is to create multilevel math centers within the classroom (see Figure 5.6). After a large group introductory lesson in a new math concept or skill, students can participate in a center that is suited to their needs—whether that be reteaching, exploration, or expansion of the skill or concept.

Students whose IEP goals in math are strictly functional typically will benefit from brief drill-and-practice sessions in a particular skill (e.g., counting objects, writing numbers, telling time, counting money), followed by applying those skills to solve functional math problems. Functional applications of math skills would include activities such as handing out the correct number of papers to each cooperative learning group, following a written or pictorial schedule, measuring ingredients for a recipe, determining the amount of money needed for a shopping trip, or counting the number of school newsletters to be distributed to each homeroom. Lengthy sessions in which isolated skills are practiced without ensuring that those skills generalize to functional contexts is generally of little benefit.

CONTENT AREAS

In some respects, adapting content area (social studies, history, science, and health) instruction may be less complicated than adapting instruction in the basic or fundamental skills. It is relatively easy to reduce the amount of content for a particular student or to reduce the complexity of the concepts to be learned. However, the reading and writing demands in the content areas can become difficult to accommodate, particularly in the upper grades. Therefore, in this section, we address strategies for adapting reading and writing demands as well as for adapting the conceptual demands of content area instruction. Once again, we emphasize the impor-

tance of being clear about the goal of instruction for the student before making decisions about instructional adaptations.

Accommodating Instruction in the Content Areas

As has been emphasized several times in this book, in order to be fully included in the life of a classroom, students with IEPs must not be merely present; they must participate actively in social and academic activities with their classmates. This requires special education and general education teachers to collaborate to design units of instruction and daily lessons that are suitable for students with a wide range of interests, abilities, and learning styles. Collaborative planning of instructional units that incorporate multiple modes and levels of instruction and rich, authentic activities for exploring concepts and practicing content-related skills and processes provides the basis of accommodating instruction in social studies and science.

Collaborative Planning of Instructional Units

How do special and general education teachers work together to plan learning activities that use multilevel curriculum and curriculum overlap? Up-front collaborative planning of instructional units assists teachers in planning for the class as a whole, while still making provisions for individual differences. Thematic units, which integrate several curriculum areas under an organizing topic, are particularly well suited to inclusive classrooms. An integrated curriculum provides a natural context from which students with differing interests and abilities can work toward curriculum objectives that vary in difficulty or come from various curriculum areas.

Many unit planning formats are available, but those recommended for use in inclusive classrooms (e.g., Fisher, Sax, & Pumpian, 1999; Schumm, Vaughan, & Harris, 1997)

Voices from the Classroom

Special education teacher Cyndi Pitonyak and the team of fifth-grade teachers with whom she worked were interested in developing ways to provide extra practice and support for fifth graders who were struggling with math concepts. However, they did not want to resort to the use of ability groups, which might negatively affect the social climate in their classrooms and prevent students from having opportunities to learn from one another.

At a team meeting, using the Issue–Action Planning format (see Figure 1.12), they identified these issues of concern:

1. We need a way to provide differentiated practice of new concepts introduced in math if we are to successfully instruct without ability grouping. Whatever we devise must be fairly easy to use.

2. We need a way to provide extra opportunity for students to master skills they did not pick up during class.

3. We need a way to increase the manipulative component of math instruction.

After generating many possible solutions to these issues, team members decided on the action they would take: They would create three math centers—the Explanations Center, the "On Your Own" Center, and the Play and Practice Center—that would keep the same format all semester and be used as a regular, second-day follow-up to whole-class introduction of new concepts and skills. Students would self-select the centers at which they would work, within guidelines for the number of students allowed at each center at the same time. Before the teachers initiated the centers, students received a careful introduction to the purpose of each center and were provided with a checklist and a folder to track their own progress through the centers.

Explanations Center

This center provided an extra opportunity for teacher-directed instruction and practice of new skills. It was essentially a repetition of the class introduction, conducted by a teacher with a small group of students. Using the overhead and white boards, students practiced solving problems together with step-by-step teacher direction.

"On Your Own" Center

This center was for use by students who understood the concept and just needed more opportunities for independent practice to improve proficiency (rate and accuracy). It essentially involved paper-and-pencil work, with keys available for self-checking.

Play and Practice Center

This center would grow as students progressed through the year. Teachers developed a couple of manipulative activities or games to go with each concept introduced. Activities were clearly labeled for the concepts they covered (e.g., "Multiplication with decimals"). Students were assigned to this center for concepts that had just been introduced or for previously covered concepts. The center included computer programs, games, and creative activities that used manipulatives instead of paper and a pencil.

At the end of the school year, Cyndi and the fifth-grade classroom teachers evaluated the math centers approach. Based on student progress and their appraisal of the practical efficiency of the approach, the team decided that this had been an effective way to address the concerns they originally had about the need for students to receive additional practice on math concepts without the use of ability grouping.

Figure 5.6.   Math centers as a strategy to allow differentiated, multilevel instruction without ability grouping. (Contributed by Cyndi Pitonyak.)

typically include 1) core unit goals for all students, with differentiated objectives for particular students; 2) multimodal, multilevel source materials; and 3) hands-on activities and creative culminating projects. As indicated on the unit plan format provided in Figure 5.7, collaborative planning of an instructional unit begins with identification of the big ideas (i.e., facts, terms, concepts, and principles), as well as the skills or processes that are essential to the topic. These are the minimal competencies that are targeted for all students in the class. Thus, the more unique skills and content that particular students will need to learn in order to make the topic meaningful and useful to them are identified. These objectives include extended or advanced objectives for students who can go beyond those minimal competencies and simplified objectives for any students who need them. One way to conceptualize adapted objectives in the content areas is to apply Bloom's (1976) taxonomy of learning objectives to the content in question. All students may learn knowledge, comprehension, and application objectives, while others also utilize the higher-order thinking skills of analysis, synthesis, and evaluation.

Next, the daily unit tasks and activities are listed, with an emphasis on designing practice activities that are hands-on and use as many input and output modalities as possible. A kick-off activity that will grab the students' interest and development of a **KWL** chart or some other technique to help students to gain access to their background knowledge about the topic and create a purpose for its study are often among the initial unit activities. The major unit projects and activities are noted (typically, some of these are cooperative group activities), along with notes about instructional adaptations that will be required for students with IEPs. From the start, the plan incorporates a variety of ways for students to participate and demonstrate learning, such as through the use of oral reports or graphic constructions instead of written reports. A collection of supplementary/alternative unit

activities also can be generated. This list can include extension activities for students who will go beyond the requirements for most students, as well as alternative activities for any student who needs them. This is also the time to designate the embedded motor, social, and communication skills that can be addressed within unit activities for students with more extensive disabilities.

To illustrate the benefits of thematic units that include many hands-on, multimodal activities, consider the unit on early American life in which Melanie and her classmates in Ms. Ramirez's fourth-grade class participated. As part of their investigation of various facets of life in the American colonies, students learned about the typical diets of the Native Americans and the early American colonists. After studying the crops that were grown and the hunting practices used, the class prepared several foods using recipes that approximated those used in the late 1600s. One group of students—Melanie and three of her classmates—made corn bread. In designing the unit, Ms. Ramirez, the three other fourth-grade teachers, and Ms. Pitonyak, the special education teacher, had identified social studies objectives as well as math objectives with varying degrees of difficulty that could be addressed during each unit activity. For most students, the cooking activities were focused on math and social studies objectives from the state fourth-grade learning standards. The general math objectives included dividing and multiplying fractions and expressing fractions in lowest terms. These objectives were practiced by having students compute how many times the recipe would need to be multiplied in order for each person in the class to have one corn muffin and then computing the amount of each ingredient required. Simplified math objectives for some students came from the second- and third-grade learning standards and included naming and comparing the fractions used in the recipe. Thus, students with these math objectives were asked to read the fractions correctly and to tell, for example, whether the recipe required more shortening or more corn meal.

Ms. Ramirez and Ms. Pitonyak also identified objectives from the functional academic,

Unit Plan

Unit Theme: _The Hometown Elementary School Courtyard Garden: Who and What Lives There?_

Teachers: _4th-Grade Team_

Dates and Times: _Monday, Wednesday, Friday at 1:00–1:50 PM, May 2–June 6, 2005_

Unit Goals: "Big Ideas" (Concepts, principles, and issues)	Minimal Competencies: (Essential facts, skills, and processes)
Interdependence of humans, other animals, plants, natural environment _Life cycles of humans, other animals, plants_ _Stewardship of the natural environment_	_Science: Scientific method, plant and animal identification and classification, animal habitats, parts of the plant, growth requirements for plants, photosynthesis, water cycle_ _Math: Measurement, graphing, decimals to two places_ _Social studies: Local/regional geography, compare/contrast, vegetation in tidewater, piedmont, and mountains_ _Art: Use of various media, history of naturalist art_

Extended/Advanced Objectives	Adapted Objectives
Math: Metric conversions of measurements _English: Greater exploration and research about naturalist literature and poetry_ _Science: Research/experimentation on growth requirements for plants_	_For Troy, Tiffany, Asa: Simplified/reduced content as per their IEPs_ _For Melanie: Content simplified to key vocabulary to use in reading, writing, spelling; embedded social, motor, and communication skills as per her IEP_

Tasks/Activities

Kick-off activity: _K-W-L chart of what we think lives in the garden. Begin inventory of plants and animals in the garden._

Lecture and demonstrations/models: _Science: Scientific method, plant and animal identification and classification, parts of the plant, growth requirements for plants, photosynthesis, water cycle. Social studies: Local/regional geography, compare/contrast vegetation in tidewater, piedmont, and mountains. Art and English: Naturalist art and literature_

Reading: _Science textbook, chapters 4–7. Social studies textbook, chapters 6, 8, 9. Novels. Poetry of nature from around the world. Read aloud after lunch._

Discussion: _Initial, weekly, and culminating discussions of K-W-L chart. Vegetation and animal life in 3 regions of state. Class meeting to plan for dedication of alpine garden._

Library/Internet research: _Choice of topics related to vegetation and animal life in 3 regions of state._

Writing: _Write descriptive paragraphs (nature journals) and poetry._

Building/Creating: _Draw/paint and photograph plants and animals across time. Plan, plant, and care for new alpine garden._

Solving: _Measurement of rainfall, temperature. Use of scientific method to study plant growth._

Culminating activity: _Dedication of alpine garden. Parents invited._

Figure 5.7.   Unit Plan.

Unit Plan *(continued)*	
Major Unit Projects (Note adaptations) *Inventory and classification of plants and animals* *Grow new plants in various subenvironments*	**Alternative or** **Supplementary Activities** *Create picture collections of appropriate plants,* *animals, and geographic features to use as text* *enhancements (Asa and Troy) or in place of* *writing projects (Melanie)*
Evaluation Measures *Science and social studies: Project booklet with* *evaluation rubric. Quizzes on plant parts and* *growth requirements.* *Math: Quiz on graphs*	**Adapted Evaluation Measures** *Adapted project booklet and rubric for Melanie*
Materials Needed *Plants for alpine garden* *Books and electronic resources:* *Drawing on nature in the classroom, grades 4–6.* *(1996). Englewood, CO: Teacher Ideas Press.* *Eyewitness encyclopedia of nature [electronic* *resource]. (1995). New York: Dorling* *Kindersley.* *Heimlich, J.E. (Ed.). (2002). Environmental* *education: A resource handbook. Bloomington,* *IN: PDK Education Foundation.* *Potter, J. (1995). Nature in a nutshell for kids:* *Over 100 activities you can do in ten minutes* *or less. New York: John Wiley & Sons.* *Raham, G. (1996). Explorations in backyard* *biology [electronic resource].* *Silver, D.M. (1993). One small square backyard.* *New York: Scientific American Books for* *Young Readers.*	**Adapted Materials Needed** *Create a picture collection of insects, small* *animals, plants of the region. Use for making* *a book or poster, sorting into categories by* *various attributes, and as writing prompts.* *Create a folder of nature and environmental* *activities from More Alternatives to* *Worksheets (Creative Teaching Press, 1994)* *to use for alternative adaptations or* *supplementary activities.*

domestic, and motor skill goal areas for certain students, particularly Melanie. Although many students in the fourth grade did not need instruction in skills such as reading the recipe and measuring ingredients using the correct measuring devices (e.g., a measuring cup for the milk, a teaspoon for the baking powder), the activity provided a functional context within which other students could work on these functional reading and math objectives. Motor skills, including pouring the milk and stirring the batter, as well as domestic skills, such as gathering and putting away the ingredients and cleaning up the cooking area, also provided instructional opportunities for some students.

During the baking activity, Melanie was able to complete the knowledge-level math objectives by responding to questions posed by Ms. Ramirez. Melanie also was able to practice her functional reading by being responsible for reading the recipe to her group. Melanie and another student in the class who has a physical disability also worked on motor skills targeted during the activity, which included pouring *milk into the measuring cup and stirring the batter. This is just one example of a unit activity that enabled Melanie and her other class-mates with and without disabilities to work to-gether in shared activities, even though their learning objectives were varied.*

Although collaborative planning of instructional units requires a significant initial investment of time, it makes adaptations more predictable in the future because many teachers use the same or similar units each year. If an entire grade-level team uses the same units, several teams' planning is assisted.

Curricular and Instructional Adaptations in the Content Areas

The primary difficulties that some students with IEPs face in their content areas are not related to their ability to comprehend the material. Instead, their listening, writing, and reading disabilities may interfere with their ability to gain access to and/or process the material. Teachers can make adaptations to listening, writing, and reading demands that will help prevent students' learning difficulties from interfering with their access to the content.

Adapting Oral Presentations or Lectures

Oral presentations or lectures can be adapted both by altering the input, or delivery, of the material and by adapting the output, or the response, required of the students. That is, teachers can assist students by adapting the format and delivery of their lectures or the requirements for listening and note taking.

Adapting the Input

- Use a guided lecture procedure: review objectives, purpose, and relevance of the material; pause frequently; pose questions; and summarize.

- Use content enhancement routines and teach students to use learning strategies for learning concepts and memorizing information (see Figure 5.8).

- Use a multisensory approach, including demonstrations, role-playing, drama, music, and pictures.

- Use visual aids (e.g., Venn diagrams, semantic maps, outlines, timelines) to illustrate topics and subtopics and how they are related.

- Keep vocabulary instruction in context.

- Explicitly teach new vocabulary and concepts:

  1. Define the new concept, giving its attributes, and if possible, show a model or picture illustrating it.

  2. Distinguish between the new concept and similar but different concepts with which it might be mistaken.

  3. Give examples and nonexamples of the concept and explain their distinguishing attributes.

  4. Present students with examples and non-examples and ask students to distinguish between the two.

  5. Have students present examples and non-examples of the concept, and have them explain their reasoning. (Graves, 2000, p. 122)

- Use temporal cues (e.g., first, next, last).

- Use controlled vocabulary; omit extraneous detail.

Adapting the Output

- Provide slot notes (see Figure 5.9). The teacher's lecture notes are printed or typed, leaving blanks or slots for the student to fill in during the lecture. Photocopies of the slot notes are made for any student who needs them, either as an ongoing IEP accommodation or as an occasional adaptation. An overhead transparency of the notes also can be made for the teacher to use to fill in the blanks as he or she lectures.

- Provide a lecture outline. The student is to check off each topic as it is covered, to circle key terms as the teacher describes them, or to copy the outline in his or her own handwriting.

What the Research Says

The University of Kansas Center for Research on Learning has developed a *strategic instruction model* that encompasses *learning strategies* for use by students and *content enhancement routines* for teachers to use in presenting content to diverse groups of students (The University of Kansas Center for Research on Learning, 2001). The learning strategies curriculum provides explicit instruction in cognitive and metacognitive skills for planning, executing, and evaluating the performance of a learning task. Learning strategies instruction provides students with a better understanding of the nature of learning tasks and the structure of knowledge and thus assists students in becoming more active and effective learners (Deshler & Schumaker, 1988; Pressley et al., 1990).

Many students—including those with typical achievement levels, those judged to be at risk for academic failure, and those with diagnosed learning disabilities—benefit from instruction that helps them to become more deliberate learners. Efficient and effective teachers and learners are strategic in their approach to learning—that is, they intentionally create tactics that will facilitate the encoding, storage, and retrieval of information. However, many students, particularly students who have learning disabilities, are not aware of their own learning needs. They therefore "need repeated instruction to understand that they must use strategies, and they need modeling before it becomes natural for them to use the strategy and to transfer [it] to other relevant settings" (Vaidya, 1999). A review of research on learning interventions supports the position that "if strategy training is carried out in a meta-cognitive, self-regulative context, in connection with specific content rather than generalized skills . . . positive results are much more likely" (Hattie, Biggs, & Purdie, 1996, p. 101). Evidence also has suggested that it is best to teach students a small repertoire of strategies that they can practice in depth over a long period of time (Pressley, 2000).

The learning strategies that have been successfully field-tested by researchers at the University of Kansas Center for Research on Learning include:

1. **Strategies related to reading, including word identification and comprehension strategies.** For example, the *visual imagery strategy* teaches students to form mental movies depicting the characters, setting, and events of narrative passages, and the *self-questioning strategy* helps students to create a purpose for reading by creating questions about the reading passage, predicting the answers, and then searching for confirmation or denial of their predictions.

2. **Strategies for storing and retrieving information.** These strategies include *first-letter mnemonics*, which can be used to memorize lists of information in any subject area and are helpful for both content knowledge (e.g., remembering historical dates and names) and procedural knowledge (e.g., the steps of the writing process or the steps for solving an equation).

3. **Strategies for expressing information.** Written expression strategies include the *paragraph writing strategy*, a strategy for organizing ideas, planning the sequence of ideas, and adding details. The *error monitoring strategy* is a proofreading and editing strategy to aid students in correcting their own work before turning it in.

The content enhancement routines (e.g., Bulgren, Deshler, & Schumaker, 1993) are systematic, field-tested methods for teachers to use to organize and present science and social studies content (although they can be adapted for use in other subject areas). For example, the *concept mastery routine* (Bulgren, Deshler, & Schumaker, 1993) gives teachers a consistent framework for defining, explaining, and giving examples of a major concept and how it relates to other concepts the students have studied.

Teachers who want to learn more about learning strategies should consult the resources listed in Appendix B. The content enhancement training and curriculum materials are available only through training offered by certified trainers.

Figure 5.8. Learning strategies and content enhancement routines.

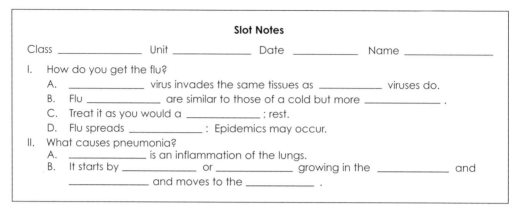

Slot Notes

Class _____ Unit _____ Date _____ Name _____

I. How do you get the flu?
    A. _____ virus invades the same tissues as _____ viruses do.
    B. Flu _____ are similar to those of a cold but more _____ .
    C. Treat it as you would a _____ ; rest.
    D. Flu spreads _____ : Epidemics may occur.
II. What causes pneumonia?
    A. _____ is an inflammation of the lungs.
    B. It starts by _____ or _____ growing in the _____ and _____ and moves to the _____ .

Figure 5.9.   Slot notes. (Contributed by Christine Burton and Johnna Elliott.)

• Provide peer note takers.

• Provide audiocassette recordings that students can listen to at home so that they can check or complete their notes.

Adapting Reading Demands

There are many ways that teachers can adapt the reading demands that are placed on students in social studies, science, and health classes so that students can learn content goals in spite of their difficulties with reading and writing. The following are ideas for making content area classes, especially those at the secondary level, more accessible for students with disabilities.

Much of the support provided in inclusive middle and high school classrooms involves supporting students in meeting the reading demands of the class. Poor or nonreaders need adaptations and accommodations that will enable them to get the needed information from their textbooks in spite of their difficulties with reading. In middle and high school, it becomes imperative to assess the reading demands in each class in which a student with reading difficulties is enrolled. It can be useful to develop a support plan for each student who is taking content area courses but needs assistance with the reading demands of the class. As shown in Figure 5.10, a Plan for Reading Adaptations and Accommodations summarizes the reading task

demands for each subject. It then lists the general adaptations and accommodations that will be necessary for each class and delineates which teacher or assistant is responsible for providing the identified supports. The special education teacher develops this plan and shares it with the classroom teacher and any instructional assistants that support students in the relevant classes.

Possible adaptations and accommodations to assist students with their textbook reading include adaptations to the instructional stimulus or input (i.e., changing the text's difficulty, amount, or format) and adaptations to the student response or output (i.e., changing the type of reading demand required of the student). Some possible adaptations and accommodations for textbook reading include the following:

• Teach the textbook's organization and structure (e.g., chapter objectives, headings and subheadings, bold and italic print, introductory and summary paragraphs, questions at the end of the chapter). In the middle and upper grades, particularly emphasize the organization of main ideas and details.

• Rewrite short passages or textbook directions at a lower level of readability.

• Have the student listen and retell what was read.

• Have the student read and then retell what he or she read.

Plan for Reading Adaptations and Accommodations for: ___Vanessa___

Subject	Reading task demand	Adaptations and accommodations	Staff
English	Silent reading of novel 20 minutes per day; novels are two grade levels above her independent level.	• Silent/oral reading group option, selected by student preference • Day readers/night readers option	Teacher/ assistant/ peer
Math	Read and follow written directions on workbook pages and worksheets.	• Worksheets: Pair symbols with direction words; rewrite directions at lower readability. • Sight word drill of direction words, two 10-minute sessions per week	Special education teacher
Science	Follow oral reading of text by classmates and teacher; identify key vocabulary; learn definitions of key vocabulary for test.	• Teacher will not call on Vanessa to read aloud. • Highlight textbook: yellow = vocabulary word, blue = definition. • Notebook: Reduce note-taking requirement to copying highlighted vocabulary words and definitions. • Tests: two study sessions prior to test; read word, find definition.	Teacher Assistant special education teacher Special education teacher

Figure 5.10.   Plan for Reading Adaptations and Accommodations. (Contributed by Christine Burton.)

- Add pictures or symbols to text.
- Provide multiple texts at various readability levels.
- Provide page and paragraph markers with simplified questions.
- Provide slot notes or a partial outline for students to complete as they read or are read to.
- Provide visual organizers such as maps, graphs, and charts for students to fill in as they read.
- For each textbook chapter for a content area class, provide a study guide of key concepts and vocabulary terms.
- Read the text aloud to the student.
- Reduce textbook information to a study guide of concepts and vocabulary.

- Use color-coded highlighting for key concepts and vocabulary (e.g., yellow for vocabulary words, blue for definitions).
- Read only highlighted key concepts and vocabulary.
- Provide supplements such as videotapes, films, CD-ROMs, and Internet resources.
- Conduct paired reading sessions.
- Allow the option of silent or oral reading groups.

Adapting Activities and Projects in the Content Areas

- Provide picture cues or an audiotape with the steps for completing a multistep task (e.g., a laboratory experiment, a job task).

- Allow the student to complete only selected steps of a social studies or science project.

- Have the student work with a peer partner.

- Reduce the writing demands. For example, give the student a word bank, fill-in-the-blank sentences, or a choice of two answers instead of requiring sentences or essays.

Alternative Adaptations in the Content Areas

Alternative adaptations for content area activities may still utilize some simplified and/or reduced unit content, but it also addresses skills from other goal areas, including embedded social, communication, motor skills, and/or basic skills in reading, writing, or math. Two key strategies to assist in devising alternative adaptations for content area activities that still maintain thematic connections with the class activity are 1) picture collections that can be used in a variety of ways and 2) lists or folders of alternative activities.

- Create picture collections related to each unit that can be used for a variety of purposes:

  1. Make a booklet and write captions for the pictures with sentences, phrases, words, or peel-off printed labels.
  2. Use the pictures as prompts for writing activities.
  3. Make a booklet with pictures and facts.
  4. Put pictures into categories by attributes (e.g., animals on one page, people on another, plants on a third).
  5. Use pictures to complete adapted versions of graphic organizers or other assignments that classmates are completing with written words (see Figure 5.11).

- Develop a list or folder of alternative activities for each unit, being sure to include a range of activities for multiple students. These activities and the necessary materials to complete them are especially helpful to have on hand during unit-related lessons that involve lengthy projects or activities that will require multiple adaptations for students with more extensive support needs. Activities can be collected from the Internet, textbooks and teaching guides, commercial workbooks, and other curriculum resources.

TESTS AND TESTING PROCEDURES

For some students with IEPs, accommodations to tests and testing procedures are the major accommodations required by their IEPs. Such testing accommodations typically include more time, no penalties for spelling, oral reading of the test, and the provision of a scribe. Students with testing accommodations are typically being tested on the same content as their classmates but are provided with accommodations intended to prevent the student's disability from interfering with his or her ability to demonstrate what he or she has learned.

When tests are adapted for students who have adapted curriculum goals, the important issue is to carefully compare the student's goals and objectives with what is being measured by the test. If the student's goals in the subject area in question are simplified, then the student may be able to take the same test as classmates but with the number of items reduced or a word bank supplied. If the student has altered curricular goals for the subject area, a paper-and-pencil test may need to be significantly adapted in format and content or even replaced by a performance task. Like other adaptations, adaptations to tests and testing procedures should seek to maximize social and instructional participation and be only as special as necessary. Figure 5.12 gives several examples of original test items, along with accommodated items that evaluate the same general curriculum goal and adapted items that evaluate a simpler but related curriculum goal.

Another way to help ensure that students' learning is accurately represented by their

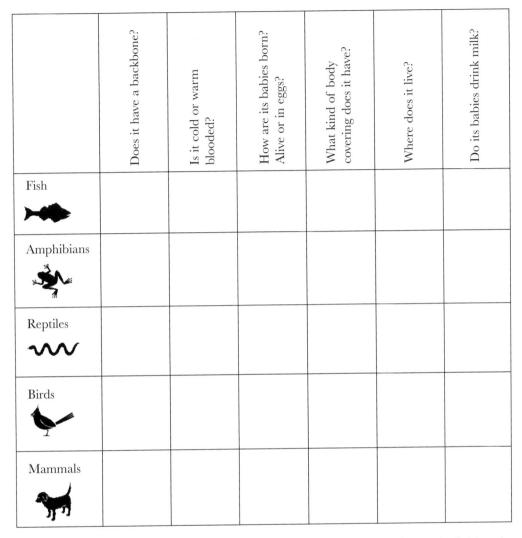

Figure 5.11. Adapted graphic organizer for an animal kingdom unit. Most students use the organizer to take notes as they read or listen to a lecture. A student with altered curriculum goals cuts out pictures of other members of each group and pastes them into the cells of the table.

test results is to teach test-taking skills. For example, teachers can explain, demonstrate, and have students practice strategies for taking multiple-choice tests. They should read all answers before selecting the best one, eliminate obviously incorrect choices, attempt all items, and do easier items first and then come back to items about which they are unsure. Strategies for taking essay tests include beginning with an outline or semantic map and planning how to allot time between drafting and revising.

Accommodating Tests and Testing Procedures

Fairly assessing student achievement in an inclusive classroom requires using multiple methods and not only paper-and-pencil tests. However, as has been stressed throughout this chapter, prior to developing alternate assessments for individual students whose learning is quite different from their typical classmates, it is important to adopt assessment measures for all students that show evidence of their

Social studies test item for most students:

General _____ and General _____ were the two opposing generals at the battle of Gettysburg.

Accommodated test item:

General _____ and General _____ were the two opposing generals at the battle of Gettysburg.

        Lee   Meade   Bragg   Jackson   Grant

Adapted test item (circle one):

General *Lee   Grant* and General *Meade   Bragg* were the two opposing generals at the battle of Gettysburg.

Science test item for most students:

All animals without backbones are called _____ .

Accommodated test item:

All animals *without* backbones are called _____ .

                vertebrates   invertebrates

Adapted test item:

Circle the invertebrate.

Figure 5.12. Accommodated and adapted test items.

progress at individualized rates. Such measures include portfolios, curriculum-based assessments, anecdotal records, peer-assisted evaluation, self-monitoring, and conferencing between the student and the teacher. In accommodating classrooms, a variety of indicators are used, progress is evaluated over time, and students learn to evaluate themselves. And as already noted, when paper-and-pencil tests are used, it is important to ensure that they are fair and appropriate in that they do not test the student's disability but test the in-

structional goals that were taught in the particular unit, chapter, or course.

Students with learning disabilities, attention disabilities, or visual impairments, or simply any student who is anxious about testing, may be better able to respond correctly if the appearance, organization, and readability of tests follow these guidelines (from Murphy, Meyers, Olesen, McKean, & Custer, 1997):

• Leave 1-inch margins on all sides.

- Double-space between test questions.

- Capitalize or underline important words.

- Place multiple-choice alternatives vertically rather than horizontally under the stem.

- Keep multiple-choice alternatives brief.

- For matching items, keep all matching items and choices on the same page.

- Include no more than 10 items on matching lists.

- Eliminate unnecessary words; use short sentences.

- Use synonyms for difficult words that are not vocabulary.

- Read the directions aloud to the class and check students' understanding of the directions.

Murphy and colleagues (1997) also provided excellent guidelines and examples for reducing the readability level of test items while still keeping the same content. Their suggestions can be used to develop tests that accommodate the reading abilities of most students in the class or to adapt a test's readability for one or more individual students.

Adapting Tests and Testing Procedures

Both testing procedures and the actual test formats used can be adapted to ensure that students' learning is fairly evaluated by a test. An array of examples follows.

- Provide a study guide.

- Use large print, or make photocopied enlargements of the class test (but include fewer items per page, so that the paper size stays the same as for the rest of the class).

- Provide a word bank for fill-in-the-blank items.

- Add picture cues to test items, or allow students to respond using pictures rather than words (see Figure 5.11)

- Rewrite directions at a lower readability level.

- Rewrite test items at a lower readability level

- Highlight important words in the directions and/or in test items.

- Provide an example for each type of test item.

- Allow students to use aids, such as a calculator, manipulatives, or charts.

- Provide a scribe for the student; the student may or may not recopy the material.

- Reduce the number of alternatives for multiple-choice items.

- For multiple-choice items, let the student circle the entire alternative, rather than the letter choice.

- Construct tiered tests. That is, write test items to fit several different levels of learning objectives. Differentiate the point value of the items at the various levels (e.g., knowledge items are worth 5 points each, application items are worth 10 points each, and analysis or synthesis items are worth 20 points each). Students may choose items to equal 100 points as long as they choose from at least two levels.

- Allow a student to prepare a chart or map instead of writing an essay.

- Provide alternative ways to demonstrate achievement that are suited to the individual students' curricular goals: projects, surveys, graphic organizers, and oral reports.

SUMMARY

In this chapter, we have described and illustrated some examples of curricular, instructional, and alternative adaptations for instructional activities in reading and writing, math, and the content areas. There are many, many more possibilities. Assuming that the

Voices from the Classroom

One way to facilitate your school's efforts to make appropriate and effective accommodations and adaptations for students is to find a way to organize the many materials and ideas that are developed and tested over time. Several of the teachers who contributed to this book have devised a system of *accommodations and adaptations notebooks* to organize the materials that they designed for students.

A large, plastic-covered, three-ring binder holds the accommodations and adaptations that have been developed for each subject area (at the elementary school level) or course (at the middle and high school levels). Each notebook is divided into two sections, one for accommodations and one for adaptations. The sections include materials such as those listed below and are kept in the school library so that any teacher or instructional assistant who needs them may borrow them.

Section I: Accommodations

- Lecture outlines
- Slot notes
- Study guides
- Tests and worksheets with accommodations, such as more space, larger print, and word banks

Section II: Adaptations

- Adapted reading material
- Picture collections
- Tests and worksheets with adaptations, such as lower readability, pictures, and diagrams

Figure 5.13.   Accommodation and adaptation notebooks.

classroom begins with a climate and culture that unites the students and teachers as an inclusive community and that accommodating curricular and instructional practices have been put into place, making these sorts of adaptations will not single out individual students as being different or stigmatize them. Students without disabilities in inclusive classrooms often learn how to assist their peers with disabilities by providing appropriate adaptations and supports in very taken-for-granted ways.

As teachers begin or continue the work of developing adaptations, they may find it help-ful to create systems that enable sharing access to the successful strategies and products across all members of the grade level or departmental team. Filing systems that organize adapted materials and other resources by subject area and grade level can enable teachers to build on their own ideas and those of their colleagues from one year to the next. Whether your filing system utilizes plastic crates, filing cabinets, or large three-ring binders (see Figure 5.13), such systems also give teachers a way to convey the adaptations they have developed to the instructional assistants or other teachers who may actually be implementing them.

References

Baker, E.T., Wang, M.C., & Walberg, H.J. (1994–1995, December–January). The effects of inclusion on learning. *Educational Leadership, 52*(4), 33–35.

Baumgart, D., Brown, L., Pumpian, I., Nisbet, J., Ford, A., Sweet, M., Messina, R., & Schroeder, J. (1982). Principle of partial participation and individualized adaptations for severely handicapped students. *Journal of The Association for Persons with Severe Handicaps, 7,* 17–27.

Bloom, B.S. (1976). *Human characteristics and school learning.* New York: McGraw-Hill.

Browder, D.M., Bambara, L.M., & Belifore, P.J. (1997). Using a person-centered approach in community-based instruction for adults with developmental disabilities. *Journal of Behavioral Education, 7,* 519–528.

Brown, L., Farrington, K., Knight, T., Ross, C., & Ziegler, M. (1999). Fewer paraprofessionals and more teachers and therapists in educational programs for students with significant disabilities. *Journal of The Association for Persons with Severe Handicaps, 24*(4), 250–253.

Brown, L., Nisbet, J., Ford, A., Sweet, M., Shiraga, B., York, J., & Loomis, R. (1983). The critical need for nonschool instruction in educational programs for severely handicapped students. *Journal of The Association for Persons with Severe Handicaps, 8*(3), 71–77.

Bulgren, J.A., Deshler, D.D., & Schumaker, J.B. (1993). *The content enhancement series: The concept mastery routine.* Lawrence, KS: Edge Enterprises.

Burke, K. (1994). *How to assess authentic learning.* Arlington Heights, IL: Skylight Training and Publishing Co.

Carnine, D. (1998). Instructional design in mathematics for students with learning disabilities. In D. Rivera (Ed.), *Mathematics education for students with learning disabilities* (pp. 119–138). Austin, TX: PRO-ED.

CAST [Center for Applied Special Technology]. *Universal design for learning.* Retrieved August 16, 2003, from http://www.cast.org/udl/

Collicott, J. (1991). Implementing multi-level instruction: Strategies for classroom teachers. In G.L. Porter & D. Richler (Eds.), *Changing Cana-* *dian schools* (pp. 191–218). North York, Ontario: The Roeher Institute.

Cunningham, P.M., & Allington, R.L. (2003). *Classrooms that work: They all can read and write* (3rd ed.). Needham Heights, MA: Allyn & Bacon.

Cunningham, P.M., Hall, D.P., & Sigmon, C.M. (1999). *The teacher's guide to the four blocks way.* Greensboro, NC: Carson-Dellosa.

Davern, L., Ford, A., Erwin, E., Schnorr, R., & Rogan, P. (1993). *Working toward inclusive schools: Guidelines for developing a building-based process to create change* [monograph]. Syracuse, NY: Syracuse University. (Special Projects/Consortium; Huntington Hall; 150 Marshall St.; Syracuse University; 13244–2340)

Deshler, D., & Schumaker, J.B. (1988). An instructional model for teaching students how to learn. In J. Graden, J. Zing, & M. Curtis (Eds.), *Alternative educational delivery systems: Enhancing instructional options for all students* (pp. 391–411). Washington, DC: National Association for School Psychologists.

Deshler, D.D., Schumaker, J.B., Marquis, J., Bulgren, J.A., Lenz, B.K., Davis, B., & Grossen, B. (2002). *The educational context and outcomes for high school students with disabilities: A case study comparing the school life of students with disabilities and their peers without disabilities.* Lawrence: Kansas University Institute for Academic Access.

Downing, J.E., Ryndak, D.L., & Clark, D. (2000, May–June). Paraeducators in inclusive classrooms: Their own perceptions. *Remedial and Special Education, 21*(3), 171–181.

Dugan, E., Kamps, D., Leonard, B., Watkins, N., Rehinberger, A., & Stackhaus, J. (1995). Effects of cooperative learning groups during social studies for students with autism and fourth-grade peers. *Journal of Applied Behavior Analysis, 28,* 175–188.

Falvey, M.A. (Ed.). (1995). *Inclusive and heterogeneous schooling: Assessment, curriculum, and instruction.* Baltimore: Paul H. Brookes Publishing Co.

Fashola, O.S., & Slavin, R.E. (1998, January). Schoolwide reform models: What works? *Phi Delta Kappan, 79*(5), 370–379.

Fennimore, T.F., & Tinzmann, M.B. (1990). *What is a thinking curriculum?* Naperville, IL: North

Central Regional Educational Laboratory (NCREL). Retrieved August 15, 2003, from http://www.ncrel.org/sdrs/areas/rpl_esys/thinking.htm

Fisher, D., Sax, C., & Pumpian, I. (1999). *Inclusive high schools: Learning from contemporary classrooms.* Baltimore: Paul H. Brookes Publishing Co.

Fisher, M., & Meyer, L.H. (2002). Development and social competence after two years for students enrolled in inclusive and self-contained educational programs. *Journal of The Association for People with Severe Handicaps, 27*(3), 165–174.

Ford, M.E. (1995). Motivation and competence development in special and remedial education. *Intervention in School and Clinic, 31,* 70–83.

Ford, A., Messenheimer-Young, T., Toshner, J., Fitzgerald, M.A., Dyer, C., Glodoski, J., & Laveck, J. (1995, July). *A team planning packet for inclusive education.* Milwaukee: Wisconsin School Inclusion Project.

Ford, A., Schnorr, R., Meyer, L., Davern, L., Black, J., & Dempsey, P. (Eds.). (1989). *The Syracuse community-referenced curriculum guide for students with moderate and severe disabilities.* Baltimore: Paul H. Brookes Publishing Co.

Forest, M., & Lusthaus, E. (1989). Promoting educational equity for all students: Circles and maps. In S. Stainback, W. Stainback, & M. Forest (Eds.), *Educating all students in the mainstream of regular education* (pp. 43–58). Baltimore: Paul H. Brookes Publishing Co.

Fryxell, D., & Kennedy, C.H. (1995). Placement along the continuum of services and its impact on students' social relationships. *Journal of The Association for Persons with Severe Handicaps, 20,* 259–269.

Gardner, H. (1983). *Frames of mind: The theory of multiple intelligences.* New York: Basic Books.

Giangreco, M.F., Broer, S.M., & Edelman, S.W. (2001). Teacher engagement with students with disabilities: Differences between paraprofessional service delivery models. *Journal of The Association for Persons with Severe Handicaps, 26*(2), 75–86.

Giangreco, M.F., Cloninger, C.J., & Iverson, V.S. (1998). *Choosing outcomes and accommodations for children (COACH): A guide to educational planning for students with disabilities* (2nd ed.). Baltimore: Paul H. Brookes Publishing Co.

Giangreco, M.F., & Doyle, M.B. (2002). Students with disabilities and paraprofessional supports: Benefits, balance, and band-aids. *Focus on Exceptional Children, 34*(7), 1–12.

Giangreco, M.F., Edelman, S., Luiselli, T.E., & MacFarland, S. (1997). Helping or hovering? Effects of instructional assistant proximity on students with disabilities. *Exceptional Children, 64*(1), 7–18.

Giangreco, M.F., & Putnam, J.W. (1991). Supporting the education of students with severe disabilities in regular education environments. In L.H. Meyer, C.A. Peck, & L. Brown (Eds.), *Critical issues in the lives of people with severe disabilities* (pp. 245–270). Baltimore: Paul H. Brookes Publishing Co.

Good, T.L., & Brophy, J.E. (1986). *Looking in classrooms* (6th ed.) New York: Harper Collins Publishers.

Graves, M.F. (2000). A vocabulary program to complement and bolster a middle-grade comprehension program. In B.M. Taylor, M.F. Graves, & P. van den Broek (Eds.), *Reading for meaning: Fostering comprehension in the middle grades* (pp. 116–135). New York: Teachers College Press.

Hattie, J., Biggs, J., & Purdie, N. (1996). Effects of learning skills interventions on student learning: A meta-analysis. *Review of Educational Research, 66*(2), 99–136.

Helmstetter, C., Peck, C., & Giangreco, M. (1994). Outcomes of interactions with peers with moderate or severe disabilities: A statewide survey of high school students. *Journal of The Association for Persons with Severe Handicaps, 19,* 263–276.

Holburn, S., & Vietze, P.M. (Eds.) (2002). *Person-centered planning: Research, practice, and future directions.* Baltimore: Paul H. Brookes Publishing Co.

Horsley, D., & Kaser, J. (1999, Fall). How to keep a change initiative on track. *Journal of Staff Development,* 40–45.

Hundert, J., Mahoney, B., Mundy, F., & Vernon, M.L. (1998). A descriptive analysis of developmental and social gains of children with severe disabilities in segregated and inclusive preschools in southern Ontario. *Early Childhood Research Quarterly, 13*(1), 49–65.

Hunt, P., Ferron-Davis, F., Beckstead, S., Curtsin, D., & Goetz, L. (1994). Evaluating the effects of placement of students with severe disabilities in general education versus special classes. *Journal of The Association for Persons with Severe Handicaps, 19*(3), 200–214.

Hunt, P., Staub, D., Alwell, M., & Goetz, L. (1994). Achievement of all students within the context of cooperative learning groups. *Journal of The Association for Persons with Severe Handicaps, 19,* 290–301.

Hunter, M. (1984). Knowing, teaching, and supervising. In P. Hosford (Ed.), *Using what we know about teaching* (pp. 169–192). Alexandria, VA: Association for Supervision and Curriculum Development.

Individuals with Disabilities Education Act (IDEA) Amendments of 1997, PL 105-17, 20 U.S.C. §§ 1400 *et seq.*

Janney, R., & Snell, M.E. (1997). How teachers use peer interactions to include students with moderate and severe disabilities in elementary general education classes. *Journal of The Association for Persons with Severe Handicaps, 21*, 72–80.

Janney, R., & Snell, M.E. (2000). *Teachers' guides to inclusive practices: Behavioral support.* Baltimore: Paul H. Brookes Publishing Co.

Janney, R.E., Snell, M.E., Beers, M.K., & Raynes, M. (1995). Integrating students with moderate and severe disabilities into general education classes. *Exceptional Children, 61*, 425–439.

Johnson, D.W., & Johnson, R. (1999). *Learning together and alone: Cooperation, competition, and individualization* (5th ed.). Needham Heights, MA: Allyn & Bacon.

Johnson, D.W., Maruyama, G., Johnson, R., Nelson, D., & Skon, L. (1981). Effects of cooperative, competitive, and individualistic goal structures on achievement: A meta-analysis. *Psychological Bulletin, 89*(1), 47–62.

Jorgensen, C.M. (1998). *Restructuring high schools for all students: Taking inclusion to the next level.* Baltimore: Paul H. Brookes Publishing Co.

Keenan, S. (1997). Program elements that support teachers and students with learning and behavior problems. In P. Zionts (Ed.), *Inclusion strategies for students with learning and behavioral problems: Perspectives, experiences, and best practices* (pp. 117–138). Austin, TX: PRO-ED.

Kennedy, C.H., Shukla, S., & Fryxell, D. (1997). Comparing the effects of educational placement on the social relationships of intermediate school students with severe disabilities. *Exceptional Children, 64*(1), 31–48.

Kincaid, D. (1996). Person-centered planning. In L.K. Koegel, R.L. Koegel, & G. Dunlap (Eds.), *Positive behavioral support* (pp. 439–465). Baltimore: Paul H. Brookes Publishing Co.

Klingner, J.K., & Vaughn, S. (1999). Students' perceptions of instruction in inclusion classrooms: Implications for students with learning disabilities. *Exceptional Children, 66*(1), 23–37.

Kovalik, S. (1997). *ITI: The model. Integrated thematic instruction* (3rd ed.). Kent, WA: Books for Educators/Susan Kovalik and Associates.

Kunc, N. (1992). The need to belong: Rediscovering Maslow's hierarchy of needs. In R.A. Villa, J.S. Thousand, W. Stainback, & S. Stainback (Eds.), *Restructuring for caring and effective education: An administrative guide to creating heterogeneous schools* (pp. 25–39). Baltimore: Paul H. Brookes Publishing Co.

Larivee, B. (1985). *Effective teaching for successful mainstreaming.* New York: Longman.

Lew, M., Mesch, D., Johnson, D. W., & Johnson, R. (1986). Components of cooperative learning: Effects of collaborative skills and academic group contingencies on achievement and mainstreaming. *Contemporary Educational Psychology, 11*(3), 229–239.

Lipsky, D.K., & Gartner, A. (1995). *The evaluation of inclusive education programs.* New York: City University of New York. National Center on Educational Restructuring and Inclusion Bulletin, 2(2).

Lipsky, D.K., & Gartner, A. (Eds.). (1997). *Inclusion and school reform: Transforming American's classrooms.* Baltimore: Paul H. Brookes Publishing Co.

Locke, E.A., & Latham, G.P. (1990). *A theory of goal setting and task performance.* Upper Saddle River, NJ: Prentice Hall.

Lou, Y., Abrami, P.C., Spence, J.D., Paulsen, C., Chambers, B., & d'Apollonio, S. (1996). Within-class grouping: A meta-analysis. *Review of Educational Research, 75*, 69–77.

Marzano, R.J. (1998). *A theory-based meta-analysis of research on instruction.* Aurora, CO: Mid-continent Research for Education and Learning. (ERIC Document Reproduction Service No. ED 427 087)

Marzano, R.J. (2000). *A new era of school reform: Going where the research takes us.* Aurora, CO: Mid-continent Research for Education and Learning (ERIC Document Reproduction Service No. ED 454 255).

Marzano, R.J. (2003). *What works in schools: Translating research into action.* Alexandria, VA: Association for Supervision and Curriculum Development.

Mastropieri, M.A., & Scruggs, T.E. (2002). *Effective instruction for special education* (3rd ed.). Austin, TX: PRO-ED.

Mastropieri, M.A., & Scruggs, T.E. (2004). *The inclusive classroom: Strategies for effective instruction* (2nd ed.). Columbus, OH: Merrill.

Mastropieri, M.A., Scruggs, T.E., Mantzicopoulos, P.Y., Sturgeon, A., Goodwin, L, & Chung, S. (1998). "A place where living things affect and depend upon each other": Qualitative and quantitative outcomes associated with inclusive science teaching. *Science Education, 82*, 163–179

McChesney, J. (1998, December). *Whole school reform.* ERIC Digest 124. Eugene: University of Oregon Clearinghouse on Educational Management.

McGregor, G., & Vogelsberg, R.T. (1998). *Inclusive schooling practices: Pedagogical and research foundations. A synthesis of the literature that informs best practices about inclusive schooling.* Baltimore: Paul H. Brookes Publishing Co.

McTighe, J., & Lyman, F.T. (1992). Mind tools for matters of the mind. In A.L. Costa, J.A. Bellanca, & R. Fogarty (Eds.), *If mind matters: Vol. 2. A forward to the future* (pp. 71–90). Palatine, IL: IR/Skylight Publishing.

Mills v. Board of Education of the District of Columbia, 348 F. Supp. 866 (D.D.C. 1972).

Mount, B., & Zwernick, K. (1988). *It's never too early, it's never too late: A booklet about personal futures planning* (Pub. No. 421-88-109). St. Paul, MN: Metropolitan Council.

Mueller, P.H., & Murphy, F.V. (2001). Determining when a student requires paraeducator support. *Teaching Exceptional Children, 33*(6), 22–27.

Murphy, D.A., Meyers, C.C., Olesen, S., McKean, K., & Custer, S.H. (1997). *Exceptions: A handbook of inclusion activities for teachers of students at grades 6–12 with mild disabilities.* Longmont, CO: Sopris West.

National Information Center for Children and Youth with Disabilities. (1998). *The IDEA Amendments of 1997* (News Digest 26). Washington, DC: Author.

National Reading Panel. (n.d.). *Report of the National Reading Panel: Teaching children to read.* Washington, DC: The National Institute of Child Health and Human Development.

Nevin, A.I., Thousand, J.S. & Villa, R.A. (1994). Achievement by all students within the context of cooperative learning groups. In J.S. Thousand, R.A. Villa, & A.I. Nevin (Eds.), *Creativity and collaborative learning: A practical guide to empowering students and teachers* (pp. 131–225). Baltimore: Paul H. Brookes Publishing Co.

No Child Left Behind Act of 2001 (PL 107-110), 20 U.S.C. §§ 6301 *et seq.*

Palincsar, A.S., & Brown, A.L. (1984). Reciprocal teaching of comprehension-fostering and comprehension-monitoring activities. *Cognition and Instruction, 1*(2), 117–175.

Peck, C.A., Carlson, P., & Helmstetter, E. (1992). Parent and teacher perceptions of outcomes for typically developing children enrolled in integrated early childhood programs: A statewide survey. *Journal of Early Intervention, 16*(1), 53–63.

Peck, C.A., Gallucci, C., Staub, D., & Schwartz, I. (1998, April). *The function of vulnerability in the creation of inclusive classroom communities: Risk and opportunity.* Paper presented at the annual meeting of the American Educational Research Association, San Diego, CA.

Pennsylvania Association for Retarded Children v. Commonwealth of Pennsylvania (PARC), 334 F. Supp. 1257 (E.D. Pa. 1972).

Peterson, M., LeRoy, B., Field, S., & Wood, P. (1992). Community-referenced learning in inclusive schools. In S. Stainback & W. Stainback (Eds.), *Curriculum considerations in inclusive classrooms* (pp. 207–227). Baltimore: Paul H. Brookes Publishing Co.

Pisha, B., & Coyne, P. (2001). Smart from the start: The promise of universal design for learning. *RASE: Remedial and Special Education, 22*(4), 197–203.

Potter, M.L. (1992). Research on teacher thinking: Implications for mainstreaming students with multiple handicaps. *Journal of Developmental and Physical Disabilities, 4*(2), 115–127.

Pressley, M. (2000). Comprehension instruction in elementary school: A quarter-century of research progress. In B.M. Taylor, M.F. Graves, & P. van den Broek (Eds.), *Reading for meaning: Fostering comprehension in the middle grades* (pp. 32–51). New York: Teachers College Press.

Pressley, M., Burkell, J., Cariglia-Bull, T., Lysynchuk, L., McGoldrick, J.A., Schneider, B., Snyder, B., Symons, S., & Woloshyn, V.E. (1990). *Cognitive strategy instruction that really improves children's academic performance.* Cambridge, MA: Brookline Books.

Pugach, M.C., & Wessen, C.L. (1995). Teachers' and students' views of team teaching of general education and learning-disabled students in two fifth-grade classes. *The Elementary School Journal, 95*(3), 279–295.

Putnam, J.W. (Ed.). (1993). *Cooperative learning and strategies for inclusion: Celebrating diversity in the classroom.* Baltimore: Paul H. Brookes Publishing Co.

Quellmalz, E., Shields, P.M., & Knapp, M.S. (1995). *School-based reform: Lessons from a national study. A guide for school reform teams.* Washington, DC: U.S. Government Printing Office. (ISBN 0-16-048415-4)

Rainforth, B., York, J., & Macdonald, C. (1992). *Collaborative teams for students with severe disabilities.* Baltimore: Paul H. Brookes Publishing Co.

Resnick, L. (Ed.). (1989). *Toward the thinking curriculum: Current cognitive research.* Alexandria, VA: Association for Supervision and Curriculum Development.

Reynolds, D., & Teddlie, C. (2000). Reflections on the critics, and beyond them. *School Effectiveness & School Improvement. 12*(1), 99–113.

Sailor, W., Gee, K., & Karasoff, P. (1993). Full inclusion and school restructuring. In M.E. Snell (Ed.), *Instruction of students with severe disabilities* (4th ed., pp. 1–30). Upper Saddle River, NJ: Merrill/Prentice Hall.

Salisbury, C.L., Palombaro, M.M., & Hollowood, T.M. (1993). On the nature and change of an inclusive elementary school. *Journal of The Association for Persons with Severe Handicaps, 18*(2), 75–84.

Sapon-Shevin, M., Ayres, B.J., & Duncan, J. (1994). Cooperative learning and inclusion. In J.S. Thousand, R.A. Villa, & A.I. Nevin (Eds.), *Creativity and collaborative learning: A practical guide to empowering students and teachers* (pp. 45–58). Baltimore: Paul H. Brookes Publishing Co.

Schumm, J.S., Vaughn, S., & Harris, J. (1997). Pyramid power for collaborative planning, *Teaching Exceptional Children, 29*(6), 62–66.

Schmoker, M.J. (1999). *Results: The key to continuous school improvement.* Alexandria, VA: Association for Supervision and Curriculum Development.

Schnorr, R.F. (1990). "Peter? He comes and goes . . .": First graders' perspectives on a part-time mainstream student. *Journal of The Association for Persons with Severe Handicaps, 15*(4), 231–240.

Scruggs, T.E., & Mastropieri, M.A. (1993). Current approaches to science education: Implications for mainstream instruction of students with disabilities. *Remedial and Special Education, 14*(1), 15–24.

Shields, P.M., & Knapp, M.S. (1997, December). The promise and limits of school-based reform: A national snapshot. *Phi Delta Kappan, 78*(4), 288–294.

Skrtic, T.M. (1991). The special education paradox: Equity as the way to excellence. *Harvard Educational Review, 61*(2), 148–206.

Slavin, R.E. (1992, February). Synthesis of research on cooperative learning. *Educational Leadership,* 71–82.

Snell, M.E. (2002, May). *Inclusion of children with high and low support needs in upper elementary classrooms.* Paper presented at the meeting of the American Association on Mental Retardation, Orlando, FL.

Snell, M.E., & Brown, F. (Eds.). (2000). *Instruction of students with severe disabilities* (5th ed.). Upper Saddle River, NJ: Merrill/Prentice-Hall.

Snell, M.E., & Janney, R. (in press). *Teachers' guides to inclusive practices: Collaborative teaming* (2nd ed.). Baltimore: Paul H. Brookes Publishing Co.

Snell, M.E., & Janney, R. (2000). *Teachers' guides to inclusive practices: Social relationships and peer support.* Baltimore: Paul H. Brookes Publishing Co.

Snell, M.E., & Macfarland, C.A. (2001, November). *Inclusion in upper elementary classrooms: A lot of it falls apart without the planning.* Paper presented at the meeting of The Association for Persons with Severe Handicaps, Anaheim, CA.

Snow, K. (2004). *People first language.* Retrieved March 15, 2004, from www.disabilityisnatural.com/peoplefirstlanguage.htm

Solomon, D., Schaps, E., Watson, M., & Battistich, V. (1992). Creating caring school and classroom communities for all students. In R. Villa, J.S. Thousand, W. Stainback, & S. Stainback (Eds.), *Restructuring for caring and effective education: An administrative guide to creating heterogeneous schools* (pp. 41–60). Baltimore: Paul H. Brookes Publishing Co.

Staub, D., & Peck, C.A. (1994–1995, December–January). What are the outcomes for nondisabled students? *Educational Leadership, 52*(4), 36–40.

Strickland, B.B., & Turnbull, A.P. (1990). *Developing and implementing individualized education programs* (3rd ed.). Columbus, OH: Merrill.

Thousand, J.S., Villa, R.A., & Nevin, A.I. (Eds.) (1994). *Creativity and collaborative learning: A practical guide to empowering students and teachers.* Baltimore: Paul H. Brookes Publishing Co.

Udvari-Solner, A. (1994). A decision-making model for curricular adaptations in cooperative groups. In J.S. Thousand, R.A. Villa, & A.I. Nevin (Eds.), *Creativity and cooperative learning: A practical guide to empowering students and teachers* (pp. 59–77). Baltimore: Paul H. Brookes Publishing Co.

Udvari-Solner, A., & Thousand, J.S. (1996). Creating a responsive curriculum for inclusive schools. *Remedial and Special Education, 17*(3), 182–192.

University of Kansas Center for Research on Learning. (2001, September). *Strategic instruction model: Learning strategies and teaching routines.* Retrieved August 15, 2003, from www.ku-crl.org/iei/sim/index.html

Vaidya, S. (1999). Metacognitive learning strategies for students with learning disabilities. *Education, 12*(1), 186–189. Retrieved August 13, 2003, from http://www.aea11.k12.ia.us/Schrader/house.htm

Van der Klift, E., & Kunc, N. (1994). Beyond benevolence: Friendship and the politics of help. In J. Thousand, R. Villa, & A. Nevin (Eds.), *Creativity and collaborative learning: A practical guide to empowering students and teachers* (pp. 391–401). Baltimore: Paul H. Brookes Publishing Co.

Vandercook, T., York, J., & Forest, M. (1989). The McGill action planning system (MAPS): A strategy for building the vision. *Journal of The Association for Persons with Severe Handicaps, 14,* 205–215.

Van Dyke, R.E., Pitonyak, C.E., & Gilley, C.T. (1996). Planning, implementing, and evaluating inclusive education within the school. In L.A. Power-deFur & F.P. Orelove (Eds.), *Inclusive education: Practical implementation of the least restrictive environment* (pp. 27–41). Gaithersburg, MD: Aspen Publishers.

Vaughn, S., Elbaum, B.E., Schumm, J., Hughes, M.T. (1998). Social outcomes for students with and without learning disabilities in inclusive classrooms. *Journal of Learning Disabilities, 31*(5), 428–436.

Vaughn, S., Gersten, R., & Chard, D.J. (2000). The underlying message in LD intervention research: Findings from research syntheses. *Exceptional Children, 67*(1), 99–114.

Villa, R.A., & Thousand, J.S. (Eds.) (2000). *Restructuring for caring and effective education: Piecing the puzzle together* (2nd ed.). Baltimore: Paul H. Brookes Publishing Co.

Voorhees, M., Landon, T., & Harvey, J. (1997). Early childhood education. In L. Power-DeFur & F. Orelove (Eds.), *Inclusive education: Practical implementation of the least restrictive environment* (pp. 131–152). Gaithersburg, MD: Aspen Publishers.

Wiggins, G., & McTighe, J. (1998). *Understanding by design.* Alexandria, VA: Association for Supervision and Curriculum Development.

Williams, L.J., & Downing, J.E. (1998). Membership and belonging in inclusive classrooms: What do middle school students have to say? *Journal of The Association for Persons with Severe Handicaps, 23*(2), 98–110.

Appendix A

Blank Forms

Team Roles and Responsibilities Checklist

Classroom _____ **Date** _____

Teaching and Support Team Members:

_____ Classroom teacher   _____ Instructional assistant

_____ Special education teacher _____ Other

x = Primary responsibility
input = Input into decision making and/or implementation

Roles and responsibilities	Who is responsible?			
	Classroom teacher	Special education teacher	Instructional assistant	Other: _____
Developing lessons/units				
Adapting curriculum				
Adapting teaching methods				
Adapting materials				
Monitoring weekly/daily student progress				
Assigning grades				
Assigning duties to/supervising assistants				
Scheduling team meetings a. IEP teams b. Core planning teams (specific students)				
Daily/weekly communication with parents				
Communication/collaboration with related services				
Facilitating peer relationships and supports				

(From Ford, A., Messenheimer-Young, T., Toshner, J., Fitzgerald, M.A., Dyer, C., Glodoski, J., & Laveck, J. [1995, July]. *A team planning packet for inclusive education.* Milwaukee: Wisconsin School Inclusion Project; adapted by permission.)

Modifying Schoolwork (2nd ed.) by Janney & Snell.

Team Survey of Inclusive Practices

School _____ Team _____ Year _____

Team Members/Roles:

_____   _____

_____   _____

_____   _____

Status Key: 3 = We have done it well.
                   2 = We have tried, but it needs improvement.
                   1 = We have not done it.

Action Priority: Indicate "high" or "low." Complete Issue-Action Plan for high-priority items.

Practice	Status (1, 2, 3)		Action Priority (high/low)	
	Date:	Date:	Date:	Date:
1. **Inclusive program model:** Do all students start from a base in general classes? Do services and supports follow the students? Does the special education model facilitate teaming?				
2. **Inclusive culture in the school:** Is diversity valued? Are we a community? Do we expect excellence and equity for all of the students?				
3. **Collaborative teaming and problem solving:** Have we identified team members' roles and responsibilities? Do we have strategies for making and communicating decisions? Do we evaluate team functioning and celebrate our successes?				
4. **Accommodating curricular and instructional practices in the classroom:** Is the curriculum meaningful? Do we use active learning; multiple modalities; and small, flexible groupings?				
5. **Strategies for making and evaluating individualized adaptations:** Do we use explicit, agreed-upon strategies for planning, delivering, and evaluating adaptations? Do adaptations facilitate social and instructional participation, and are they only as special as necessary?				
6. **Strategies to facilitate peer relationships and supports:** Do we teach social interaction and problem-solving skills? Do we facilitate social and helping relationships for all students?				

(From Ford, A., Messenheimer-Young, T., Toshner, J., Fitzgerald, M.A., Dyer, C., Glodoski, J., & Laveck, J. [1995, July]. *A team planning packet for inclusive education.* Milwaukee: Wisconsin School Inclusion Project; adapted by permission.)

Modifying Schoolwork (2nd ed.) by Janney & Snell.

Issue–Action Plan

Student/Team _____ **Date** _____

Team Members Present _____

_____

RE _____

_____

_____

Issue	Planned action	Who is responsible?

Steps and Tools for Planning Individualized Adaptations

Step 1. Gather Information

    a. About the Student
- ❏ Student Information Form (confidential)
- ❏ Program-at-a-Glance

    b. About the Classroom
- ❏ General Assessment of Classroom Activities
- {❏} Ecological Assessment of Classroom Activities

Step 2. Determine When Adaptations Are Needed
- ❏ General Assessment of Classroom Activities
- {❏} Program Planning Matrix

Step 3. Decide on Planning Strategies
- ❏ Guide to Adaptation Planning Strategies

Step 4. Plan and Implement Adaptations: First General, Then Specific

    a.
- ❏ Adaptations Plan and/or
- {❏} Classroom Participation Plan with General Adaptations

    b.
- ❏ Weekly Plan for Specific Adaptations (elementary or secondary)

Step 5. Plan and Implement Alternative Adaptations

Step 6. Monitor and Evaluate
- ❏ Team Meeting Agenda and Minutes
- ❏ Team Evaluation of Student Adaptations

Key: {❏} indicates tools typically used only for students with severe disabilities. Most often, these are students who have extensive support needs and significant curricular adaptations.

Student Information Form (Confidential)

Student _____ Grade _____ School Year _____

Current Teachers _____ Last Year's Teachers _____

Special Education & Related Services ____ Academics (list) ____ Speech: ____ Occupational therapy: ____ Physical therapy: ____ Aide support: ____ Sp. ed. instruction: ____ Sp. ed. consultation: ____ Other:	**Likes** **Dislikes**
Medical/health ____ Medication ____ Allergies ____ Diabetes ____ Seizures ____ Other medical/physical needs:	**See guidance counselor/ principal for other relevant confidential information?** ____ yes ____ no **Behavior Plan?** ____ yes (attach) ____ no **SOL Testing Accommodations?** ____ yes ____ no **Type of diploma** _____
What works/learns best when ____ Seeing (needs picture/graphic organizer) ____ Hearing and doing (teacher modeling) ____ Moving (hands-on work, labs, field trips) ____ Getting multisensory input (all of the above)	**Other important information/ areas of concern**

Program-at-a-Glance

Student _____ **Date** _____

IEP goals	IEP accommodations

Academic/ social management needs	Comments/special needs

General Assessment of Classroom Activities

Subject/Grade Level _____ Date _____

Student _____ Teacher _____

Instructional Activities		
Typical activities	**Frequently used student responses/tasks**	**Adaptations?**
Whole class		
Small groups		
Independent		
Homework (frequency and approximate duration)		
Textbooks, other frequently used materials		
General education teacher assistance		
Evaluation/testing Test/quiz format Sources of information for tests		
Classroom rules and contingencies		
Norms for student interaction and movement		
Procedures for routines		

(Contributed by Johnna Elliott and Cyndi Pitonyak.)

Modifying Schoolwork (2nd ed.) by Janney & Snell. Copyright © 2004 Paul H. Brookes Publishing Co.

Ecological Assessment of Classroom Activities

Teacher _____ **Grade** _____ **Student** _____

Subject _____ **Activity** _____ **Time** _____ **Date** _____

Typical sequence of steps/procedures	Target student participation

Skills needed to increase participation

Adaptations needed to increase participation

Program Planning Matrix

Student _____ Class _____ Date _____

Class Schedule

IEP GOALS									

(Key: *x* = Instruction provided; O = Classroom Participation Plans with General Adaptations required; ● = General Adaptations Plan and Weekly Plan for Specific Adaptations required)

Guide to Adaptation Planning Strategies (Individual)

Student _____ Class _____ Date _____

Classroom Teacher _____ Special Education Teacher _____

Meetings: When? _____ How Long? _____

Planning Format:

How will objectives be adapted?   ____ Simplified   ____ Altered (functional/
                                                              embedded skills)

Materials to be adapted:

____ textbook   ____ homework   ____ worksheet ____ study guides ____ quizzes/tests

____ other:

Plan for exchanging materials that need to be adapted:

Default plan: What will we do if either of us defaults on our responsibilities?
  Special education teacher:

  Classroom teacher:

Additional comments:

(Contributed by Johnna Elliott and Cyndi Pitonyak.)

Modifying Schoolwork (2nd ed.) by Janney & Snell. Copyright © 2004 Paul H. Brookes Publishing Co.

Guide to Adaptation Planning Strategies (Classroom)

Class _____ Semester/Year _____

Classroom Teacher _____ Special Education Teacher _____

Meetings: When? _____ How Long? _____

Plan for exchanging materials (who gives what to whom and by when):

Plan for if either teacher defaults on responsibilities:

Students with IEPs	Adapted curriculum?	Format for adaptation plans			Materials to be adapted					
		Classroom participation plans	Individualized adaptations plan	Weekly plan for specific adaptations	Textbooks	Worksheets	Homework	Quizzes/tests	Study guides	Other:

Individualized Adaptations Plan

Student _____ Class _____ Date _____

Classroom Teacher _____ Special Education Teacher _____

Objectives: _____

_____

Class activity	General adaptations	Specific adaptations[*]

[*] Specific adaptations developed during the weekly planning meeting.
(Contributed by Johnna Elliot.)

Modifying Schoolwork (2nd ed.) by Janney & Snell. Copyright © 2004 Paul H. Brookes Publishing Co.

Classroom Participation Plan with General Adaptations

Student _____ **Class** _____ **Date** _____

Curricular Adaptations _____

Activity	IEP goals	General adaptations and procedures

Weekly Plan for Specific Adaptations (Elementary)

Student _____ Teacher/Class _____ Week of _____ Unit Theme _____

Subjects	Class objectives	Activities	Specific adaptations

Modifying Schoolwork (2nd ed.) by Janney & Snell. Copyright © 2004 Paul H. Brookes Publishing Co.

Weekly Plan for Specific Adaptations (Secondary)

Student _____ Plan for Week of _____

Teacher _____ Class _____

Class activity	Specific adaptations

Checklist of General Adaptations

Student _____ Teacher _____ Grade _____ Date _____

Note: Use one page for each class activity (elementary) or for each class (middle or high school).

Class activity or course/time	Okay as is?	Adaptations needed	
		General adaptations (include a brief description)	**Specific adaptations (planned weekly)**
		☐ Curriculum goals ☐ Textbook ☐ Materials ☐ Tests ☐ Cuing/Feedback ☐ Physical environment ☐ Personal support ☐ Alternate activity ☐ Other	

Team Meeting Agenda and Minutes

Student _____ **Teacher/Grade** _____ **Date** _____

People Present _____

_____

_____

Agenda Items/Decisions

Next Meeting

Date: _____ **Time:** _____ **Who:** _____

Agenda Items:

Team Evaluation of Student Adaptations

Student _____ **Class** _____ **Date** _____

Team Member(s) Completing Form _____

Yes	No	Questions about the student's adaptations
		1. I am clear about my role in designing and implementing adaptations.
		2. Decisions about adaptations are based on criteria that have been agreed on by the team.
		3. We have a system for solving problems related to the student's progress, behavior, and adaptations.
		4. The student receives adequate and appropriate in-class support.
		5. The student's curricular and instructional adaptations are only as special as necessary.
		6. The adaptations enable the student to participate actively in class activities with peers.
		7. The student receives adequate instruction and practice in IEP goals/objectives.
		8. I am satisfied with the student's progress on IEP goals/objectives.
		9. The student's alternative activities are appropriate and do not prevent him or her from being a full member of the class.
		10. The student has a variety of positive relationships with peers.

Modifying Schoolwork (2nd ed.) by Janney & Snell. Copyright © 2004 Paul H. Brookes Publishing Co.

Appendix B

Resources on Designing
Schoolwork for Inclusive Classrooms

CREATING AN EFFECTIVE AND INCLUSIVE SCHOOL CULTURE

Brandt, R.S. (1996). Creating a climate for learning [topical issue]. *Educational Leadership, 54*(1).

Developmental Studies Center. (1994). *At home in our schools: A guide to schoolwide activities that build community.* Oakland, CA: Author.

Developmental Studies Center. (1996). *Ways we want our class to be: Class meetings that build commitment to kindness and learning.* Oakland, CA: Author.

Kohn, A. (1996). *Beyond discipline: From compliance to community.* Alexandria, VA: Association for Supervision and Curriculum Development.

Kreidler, W.J. (1984). *Creative conflict resolution: More than 200 activities for keeping peace in the classroom.* Glenview, IL: Scott, Foresman & Company.

Sergiovanni, T.J. (1994). *Building community in schools.* San Francisco: Jossey-Bass.

Solomon, D., Schaps, E., Watson, M., & Battistich, V. (1992). Creating caring school and classroom communities for all students. In R. Villa, J.S. Thousand, W. Stainback, & S. Stainback (Eds.), *Restructuring for caring and effective education* (pp. 41–60). Baltimore: Paul H. Brookes Publishing Co.

Van Dyke, R.E., Pitonyak, C.E., & Gilley, C.T. (1996). Planning, implementing, and evaluating inclusive education within the school. In L.A. Power-deFur & F.P. Orelove (Eds.), *Inclusive education: Practical implementation of the least restrictive environment* (pp. 27–41). Gaithersburg, MD: Aspen Publishers.

Villa, R.A., & Thousand, J.S. (Eds.). (2000). *Restructuring for caring and effective education: Piecing the puzzle together* (2nd ed.). Baltimore: Paul H. Brookes Publishing Co.

ACCOMMODATING CURRICULUM

Kovalik, S. (1997). *ITI: The model. Integrated thematic instruction* (3rd ed.). Kent, WA: Books for Educators/Susan Kovalik and Associates.

Marzano, R.J., Brandt, R.S., Hughes, C.S., Jones, B.F., Presseisen, B.Z., Rankin, S.C., & Suhor, C. (1988). *Dimensions of thinking.* Alexandria, VA: Association for Supervision and Curriculum Development.

ACCOMMODATING INSTRUCTIONAL PRACTICES: ACTIVE LEARNING, MULTIMODAL APPROACHES, LEARNING STRATEGIES, COOPERATIVE LEARNING, AND PEER TUTORING

Armstrong, T. (2000). *Multiple intelligences in the classroom.* Alexandria, VA: Association for Supervision and Curriculum Development.

CAST [Center for Applied Special Technology]. (2001). *Summary of universal design for learning concepts.* Retrieved August 16, 2003, from www.cast.org/udl

Cohen, E.G. (1994). *Designing group work: Strategies for the heterogeneous classroom.* New York: Teachers College Press.

Delequandri, J., Greenwood, C.R., Whorton, D., Carter, J.J., & Hall, R.V. (1986). Classwide peer tutoring. *Exceptional Children, 52,* 535–542.

Dunn, R., & Dunn, K. (1992). *Teaching secondary students through their individual learning styles.* Needham Heights, MA: Allyn & Bacon.

Harmin, M. (1994). *Inspiring active learning.* Alexandria, VA: Association for Supervision and Curriculum Development.

Hyerle, D. (1996). *Visual tools for constructing knowledge.* Alexandria, VA: Association for Supervision and Curriculum Development.

Johnson, D.W., & Johnson, R. (1999). *Learning together and alone: Cooperation, competition, and individualization* (5th ed.). Needham Heights, MA: Allyn & Bacon.

Kovalik, S. (1997). *ITI: The model. Integrated thematic instruction* (3rd ed.). Kent, WA: Books for Educators/Susan Kovalik and Associates.

Marzano, R.J., Pickering, D.J., & Pollock, J.E. (2001). *Classroom instruction that works: Research-based strategies for increasing student achievement.* Alexandria, VA: Association for Supervision and Curriculum Development.

Mastropieri, M.A., & Scruggs, T.E. (2000). *The inclusive classroom: Strategies for effective instruction.* Columbus, OH: Merrill.

Pressley, M., Burkell, J., Cariglia-Bull, T., Lysynchuk, L., McGoldrick, J.A., Schneider, B., Snyder, B., Symons, S., & Woloshyn, V.E. (1990). *Cognitive strategy instruction that really improves children's academic performance.* Cambridge, MA: Brookline.

Putnam, J.W. (Ed.). (1998). *Cooperative learning and strategies for inclusion: Celebrating diversity in the classroom* (2nd ed.). Baltimore: Paul H. Brookes Publishing Co.

Renzulli, J.S., Leppien, J.H.H., & Hays, T.S. (2000). *The multiple menu model: A practical guide for developing differentiated curriculum.* Mansfield Center, CT: Creative Learning Press.

Slavin, R.E. (1990). *Cooperative learning: Theory, research, and practice.* Boston: Allyn & Bacon.

Tomlinson, C.A. (1995). *How to differentiate instruction in mixed-ability classrooms.* Alexandria, VA: Association for Supervision and Curriculum Development.

SOFTWARE FOR GRAPHIC ORGANIZERS

Makes Sense Strategies: http://www.bamaed.ua.edu/mindmaps/free_downloads.htm

Inspiration Software: http://www.academicsuperstore.com/index.html?

Masterminds Publishing: http://www.graphicorganizers.com

Masterminds: http://www.ldonline.org/ld_store/masterminds.html

North Central Regional Educational Laboratory (NCREL): http://www.ncrel.org/sdrs/areas/issues/students/learning/lr1grorg.htm

LITERACY INSTRUCTION IN INCLUSIVE CLASSROOMS

Allington, R.L., & Cunningham, P.M. (1996). *Schools that work: Where all children read and write.* New York: Addison-Wesley Longman.

Cunningham, P.M., & Allington, R.L. (2003). *Classrooms that work: They can all read and write* (3rd ed.). Needham Heights, MA: Allyn & Bacon.

Fountas, I.C., & Pinnell, G.S. (2001). *Guiding readers and writers (Grades 3–6): Teaching comprehension, genre, and content literacy.* Portsmouth, NH: Heinemann.

Mastropieri, M.A., & Scruggs, T.E. (2000). *The inclusive classroom: Strategies for effective instruction* (pp. 411–456). Columbus, OH: Merrill.

Parry, J., & Hornsby, D. (1985). *Write on: A conference approach to writing.* Portsmouth, NH: Heinemann.

PUBLISHING COMPANIES FEATURING HIGH-INTEREST/LOW VOCABULARY FICTION AND NONFICTION BOOKS

Globe Fearon (adapted classics and nonfiction)

Pendulum Press (mysteries)

Steck-Vaughn (fiction and nonfiction)

New Reader's Press (adapted classics and nonfiction)

Lakeshore (illustrated, adapted classics and nonfiction)

INDIVIDUALIZED ADAPTATIONS, ACCOMMODATIONS, AND ALTERNATIVE INSTRUCTION

Elliott, J.R. (1996). Strategies for including students in elementary school programs. In L.A. Power-deFur & F.P. Orelove (Eds.), *Inclusive education: Practical implementation of the least restrictive environment* (pp. 153–166). Gaithersburg, MD: Aspen Publishers.

Falvey, M.A. (1995). *Inclusive and heterogeneous schooling: Assessment, curriculum, and instruction.* Baltimore: Paul H. Brookes Publishing Co.

Giangreco, M.F., Cloninger, C.J., & Iverson, V.S. (1998). *Choosing outcomes and accommodations for children (COACH): A guide to educational planning for students with disabilities* (2nd ed.). Baltimore: Paul H. Brookes Publishing Co.

Murphy, D.A., Meyers, C.C., Olesen, S., McKean, K., & Custer, S.H. (1997). *Exceptions: A handbook of inclusion activities for teachers of students at grades 6–12 with mild disabilities.* Longmont, CO: Sopris West.

Peterson, M., LeRoy, B., Field, S., & Wood, P. (1992). Community-referenced learning in inclusive schools. In S. Stainback & W. Stainback (Eds.), *Curriculum considerations in inclusive class-*

rooms (pp. 207–227). Baltimore: Paul H. Brookes Publishing Co.

Rainforth, B., & York-Barr, J. (1997). *Collaborative teams for students with severe disabilities: Integrating therapy and educational services* (2nd ed.). Baltimore: Paul H. Brookes Publishing.

Ryndak, D.L., & Alper, S. (Eds.). (2003). *Curriculum content for students with significant disabilities in inclusive settings* (2nd ed.). Needham Heights, MA: Allyn & Bacon.

ALTERNATIVE AND ADAPTED EVALUATION PROCEDURES

Brandt, R. (1996–1997). On authentic performance assessment [topical issue]. *Educational Leadership, 54*(4).

Burke, K. (1994). *How to assess authentic learning.* Arlington Heights, IL: Skylight Training and Publishing.

Index

Page numbers followed by *f* indicate figures; those followed by *t* indicate tables.